the
Elder s
handbook

By Louis M. Tamminga

FAITH
ALIVE®
Christian Resources

Grand Rapids, Michigan

The Elder's Handbook by Louis M. Tamminga. © 2009 by Faith Alive Christian Resources, 2850 Kalamazoo Ave. SE, Grand Rapids, MI 49560. This book is a revision of *Guiding God's People in a Changing World: A Handbook for Elders*, Faith Alive Christian Resources, 1998.

We welcome your comments. Call us at 1-800-333-8300 or e-mail us at editors@ faithaliveresources.org.

Library of Congress Cataloging-in-Publication Data
Tamminga, Louis M.
The elder's handbook / by Louis M. Tamminga.
     p. cm.
ISBN 978-1-59255-460-7 (alk. paper)
1. Christian Reformed Church—Government—Handbooks, manuals, etc. 2. Elders (Church officers)—Christian reformed Church—Handbooks, manuals, etc. I. Title.
BX6826.T35 2009
253—dc22

                                                        2008036838

10 9 8 7 6 5 4 3 2

to Jean

companion in caring

Contents

Part 4: Council and Consistory

Part 5: Beyond the Local Church

Preface

This book is about elders and for elders. It reflects many years of working side by side with elders, not only as a pastor but as an elder myself. This is a how-to book of sorts, but I hope you will find it more than that.

The apostle Paul wrote, "Here is a trustworthy saying: Whoever aspires to be an overseer desires a noble task" (1 Tim. 3:1). When you were elected and ordained to be an elder (overseer) in your church, you probably felt more trepidation than Paul seems to admit. But if this handbook will help you to fulfill this noble task more effectively, both the church and you yourself will be the richer for it. In the end may God receive your thanks for having called you to serve in this special task.

This book contains five parts:

- ▶ Part 1 provides a brief biblical background to the office of elder and offers some general observations on the concept of "office."

- ▶ Part 2 focuses on you, the person who has accepted God's call to serve as elder. It discusses the nature of calling, how you can prepare yourself for the tasks ahead, what gifts are needed, how you can increase your skills, and so on.

- ▶ Part 3 considers your ministry to the individuals entrusted to your care.

- ▶ Part 4 explores the ministry of the consistory and council as they serve the congregation and oversee the programmatic part of church life.

- ▶ Part 5 consists of a brief survey of your church beyond the contours of denominational life.

Read this book to sharpen your skills as an elder, and reread certain sections as needs arise in your work (see the topical index). This book can also be used for group study in council meetings, elders' conferences, or training sessions for new elders.

I want to thank the dozens of elders and pastors—too many to acknowledge individually here—who afforded me the benefit of their observations and suggestions, helping to shape the revised edition of this *Elder's Handbook*.

—L.M.T.

The Office of Elder in the Bible

We'll begin by seeing what the Old and New Testaments have to teach us about the office of elder. Then we'll examine the kinds of activities elders did and make some general observations about the offices of the church. The office you hold in the church is a venerable one that comes with God's special promises.

1. Leaders among God's Old Testament People

The Bible's earliest references to elders are found in the book of Exodus. When Israel was a small, struggling nation held in slavery in Egypt, God placed elders—leaders of families and tribes—among the people. Although we don't know if their office was specifically instituted, we do know that Moses relied on their wisdom and understanding.

Elders in the Old Testament were leaders among God's people in good times and in bad. They were not afraid to take risks. They accompanied Moses on his repeated trips to Pharaoh and helped Moses lead Israel through desert wanderings to the Promised Land. As the years went by, Moses increasingly depended on their help.

Here are just a few examples of some of the responsibilities elders assumed:

▶ Moses appointed some elders to be rulers in Israel (Ex. 18:24-25).

▶ Moses sought their advice before going to Pharaoh to negotiate the Israelites' exodus from Egypt (Ex. 4:29).

▶ Moses selected seventy elders to accompany him on special missions (Ex. 24:1-11; Num. 11:16).

▶ Elders were appointed as judges to dispense justice, sometimes in very complex situations (Deut. 21:1-9).

▶ Later, elders heard civil cases as they sat in the city gate (Josh. 20:4).

▶ They were liturgical leaders (Deut. 31:9).

▶ Elders were called upon to enforce the law (Deut. 27:1).

▶ Elders helped the people by settling disputes (Deut. 25:7-10).

▶ Some elders were called to participate in ceremonies celebrating the forgiveness of sins (Lev. 4:15).

During the chaotic years of the judges, the elders were the last resort of reason, protection, and stability for many people. Their absence from the city gate when their services were most needed was a chilling judgment on the city of Jerusalem

(Lam. 5:14). At the time of Jesus' birth, elders occupied a prominent place in the religious world. But because most of them lacked the spiritual foresight to celebrate his coming, God raised up other leaders such as Simeon and Anna to welcome the Savior.

The task of elders was not easy then; it is no easier now. Elders sometimes failed then; they sometimes fail now. But God used them then and continues to use them today. In the Old Testament, the elders kindled messianic hope in the hearts of God's people. Today elders encourage the people they shepherd to magnify the Messiah in their lives.

2. Leaders in Christ's New Testament Church

As is true in the Old Testament, the New Testament gives few details about the institution of the office of elder. The book of Acts simply reports that there were elders in the local churches. The church in Jerusalem was likely the first to have elders. When there was a famine in that part of the world, Barnabas and Saul delivered aid from the churches in the outlying regions into the hands of the elders at Jerusalem (Acts 11).

Soon after, perhaps inspired by this good provision in the church of Jerusalem, Paul and Barnabas "appointed elders for them in each church" (Acts 14:23). Later Paul instructed Titus to "appoint elders in every town" (Titus 1:5). These appointments had a deeper dimension. Paul pointed out later that the offices were a gift from Christ to the churches (Eph. 4:11-16). Elders today also assume their office by divine appointment.

Responsibilities

The New Testament describes the wide variety of tasks performed by elders:

▶ When problems arose—as they always do when churches grow—the elders searched the will of God for solutions (Acts 15:5-6).

▶ They assisted the apostles—who had the unique task of laying the foundation of the New Testament church—and consoled them with tears of empathy (Acts 20:37).

▶ They ordained gifted church workers to offices connected with specific tasks (1 Tim. 4:14).

▶ They "directed the affairs" of the churches (1 Tim. 5:17).

▶ They prayed with parishioners for healing (James 5:14).

▶ They preached and taught (1 Tim. 5:17).

"Have confidence in your leaders and submit to their authority, because they keep watch over you as those who must give an account. Do this so that their work will be a joy, not a burden, for that would be of no benefit to you."

—*Hebrews 13:17*

Names

Two words in the original Greek are translated as "elder": *presbuteros* and *episcopos*. *Presbuteros*, from which our word "presbyter" comes, refers to an older person who has acquired wisdom with age. *Episcopos*, or "bishop," refers to the elder's function as an overseer of God's people.

Another common designation is "shepherd." Both Paul and Peter urged the elders to be shepherds. Paul said the elders are to "be shepherds of the church of God, which he bought with his own blood" (Acts 20:28). And Peter urged the elders to be "shepherds of God's flock" (1 Pet. 5:2).

You too are called by God to be a shepherd to his flock. The responsibilities and tasks of that calling will fill the rest of this book.

Elders work in tandem with the ministers of the church. Remember that all offices have the same dignity (Church Order, Art. 2). And elders are often more directly acquainted with life's daily problems than the pastors.

The Shepherd

In many congregations the pastor is thought to be the shepherd, and that is true. But it's important to remember that the elder's role as shepherd is at least as important as the pastor's.

3. Some Thoughts on "Office"

Adam

Officebearing is deeply rooted in the human race. Adam was created in true *knowledge, holiness,* and *righteousness,* which he expressed through his three-fold office of *prophet, priest,* and *king.* Adam knew the will of God as the prophet, he was devoted to God as the priest, and he represented God in creation as the king. Because of the fall into sin, Adam and all of humankind were no longer able to devote their lives to God. Rather than serving the Creator God, they sought to serve themselves.

Christ

The Bible introduces Christ as the "second" or "last" Adam (1 Cor. 15:45; Rom. 5:12-17). He became the Savior of Adam's helpless race by virtue of his three-fold office: *prophet* (Luke 1:76; 7:16; 13:33), *priest* (Heb. 7:11-17; 8:11-12; 13:1-2), and *king* (1 Tim. 1:17; 6:15; Luke 19:38). As Prophet he reveals to us the counsel and will of God for our deliverance; as Priest he sets us free from sin by his sacrifice; and as King he governs us by his Word and Spirit and guards and keeps us (Heidelberg Catechism, Q&A 31). The leaders of the Old Testament people of Israel held corresponding offices: *prophets* who spoke on God's behalf, *kings* who ruled on God's behalf, and *priests* who mediated between God and the people through the system of prayers and sacrifices. All these offices are fulfilled in the coming of Christ, the Messiah, and in him these three offices were once again perfectly united.

Believers

Believers are anointed in Christ to share these offices with him in the fullness of their lives. As prophets they confess his name and know his will; as priests they present themselves as living sacrifices of thanks and dedication; and as kings they do their Father's will and strive with good conscience against the devil (Heidelberg Catechism, Q&A 32). This three-fold office, which all believers share, is called the "office of all believers."

Note: Section 20 will refer to pastoral calls and family visiting as the prime task of the elders. But note that all believers are officebearers in their own right. They can and must minister to each other. Elders, deacons, and ministers take the lead role, which means that they recruit the members to minister to the members. This is important. The number of elders tends to be too large in many churches. By engaging the membership in the visiting challenge, consistories can be limited to men and women especially gifted for their office. Some churches now have visiting teams (pastoral care task forces) composed of gifted members who are not elders.

Special Offices and Word Ministry

It is the calling of Christ's church on earth to build, equip, and encourage its members to exercise this *office of all believers* in their daily lives, privately and publicly (Eph. 4:22-24).

In order to do that effectively, the church needs leaders. These leaders hold the "special offices" of *elder, deacon,* and *minister*. Their authority in exercising these offices is limited to the instituted church and is grounded in the authority of Christ, who is the Head of the Church (Eph. 1:15-23).

> "But you are a chosen people, a royal priesthood, a holy nation, God's special possession, that you may declare the praises of him who called you."
>
> —1 Peter 2:9

Note that there is a parallel between Christ's three-fold office and that of the three special offices in the church. The *ministerial* office focuses on the prophetic exposition of God's will in Christ for our salvation, the office of *deacon* focuses in a priestly way on blessing those in need, and the office of *elder* represents Christ's royal authority in ruling and caring for the church.

> **Study Source**
> You'll find a wealth of helpful material regarding the concept of office in the *Acts of Synod 1973*, Report 44.

But bear in mind that these three offices of prophet, priest, and king were not meant to be continued in the New Testament church. The traditional three-fold New Testament offices became more and more integrated into one unified ministry of the Word. The New Testament church proclaims the Word of salvation, is governed by the Word, and does the work of mercy as an expression of the Word in deed. And there is often a functional overlap between these three offices.

▶ Acts 6:1-7 describes the appointment of seven helpers in the church's ministry. It is often thought that their office closely resembled that of deacons. But two of them, Philip and Stephen, were soon engaged in the proclamation of the gospel. In fact, in Acts 21:8, Philip is called "the evangelist."

▶ Paul's activities in Romans 15:25-26 seem to be quite diaconal, ministering as he did to the poor of Jerusalem.

The deacon's work is always very pastoral; the local minister is often involved in matters of governing the church, and the elder teaches the gospel as he or she visits church members and others. The secret is that the three church offices cooperate in leading the congregation in full-orbed biblical living. The overall ministry of a local church can be seen as a triangle with each of the three offices occupying one of the three angles.

Ephesians 4:11 speaks of five offices. The first two, *apostles* and *prophets,* were temporary; they revealed God's Word before the Scriptures were written down. Those offices ended with the closing of the apostolic age. The next three, *evangelists*, *pastors*, and *teachers*, all labored in Word ministry and as such continue among us today in the offices of elder and minister.

Ministry Associates

In 1978 synod created the office of *ministry associate* (originally called *evangelist*) in addition to the original three offices (Church Order, Art. 23). It was considered less a fourth office than a component of the office of pastor. Synod 1995 adopted a revision of the Church Order by adding Article 23c, which states that the ministry associate "may also serve an organized congregation along with a

Bible Passages

Here are some Bible texts that refer to the office of elder. A careful reading will help you form a general idea of how the Lord used the office of elder to build the church.

- Matthew 18:17-18
- John 20:23
- Acts 6:1-7
- Acts 11:27-30
- Acts 14:23
- Acts 20:17-31
- Acts 21:8
- Romans 12:8
- Romans 15:26
- 1 Corinthians 12:27-30

- 2 Corinthians 5:16-21
- Ephesians 4:11-13
- Philippians 1:1
- 1 Timothy 3:1
- 1 Timothy 5:17
- 2 Timothy 2:2
- 2 Timothy 3:10
- Titus 1:5-9
- Hebrews 7:11-17
- 1 Peter 5:2-3

minister of the Word." And Synod 2001 added that those who serve in "ministries such as education, evangelism, music, and ministries to children, youth, adults, and others within or outside of the congregations" are to be acknowledged as elders of their calling churches. They also have the privilege of administering the sacraments.

Calvin's Geneva

Following the Middle Ages, the churches of the sixteenth-century Reformation placed renewed emphasis on the office of elder. Swiss reformer John Calvin (1509-1564) took issue with the Roman Catholic view of the office of priest. In the Roman church the priest's ministry was centered in the Mass, which represented a repetition of the sacrifice of Christ on the cross. Instead, Calvin focused on the Word ministry of the New Testament officebearers by which believers were restored to a relationship of faith in Jesus Christ, who "sacrificed for their sins once for all when he offered himself"(Heb. 7:27).

Calvin distinguished between the *ruling elder* and the *teaching elder*. The latter evolved into the office of minister. Calvin's church in Geneva also instituted the office of deacon, which Calvin spoke of with much appreciation.

It was also Calvin who introduced regular elders' visits to the members in their homes. For Calvin such visits replaced the sacrament of penance of the church of the Middle Ages. "The church to the people, instead of the people to the church" (Eugene Hedeman).

The way the offices functioned in the churches of Geneva became a model for the churches of the Reformation elsewhere in Europe.

Calvin also spoke of the office of "doctor." Doctors taught the ministerial students in the university. It too was an aspect of the office of minister of the Word.

Calvin avoided defining the church offices too narrowly and pleaded for the churches to have leaders who proclaimed the Word of God. In that, he followed Scripture, which nowhere gives exact definitions of the separate offices but describes the activities in which these officebearers were engaged.

The Well-Equipped Servant

Part 2 focuses on you, the person who has accepted the office of elder. In Part 2 we discuss the nature of calling, how you can prepare yourself for the tasks ahead, what gifts are needed, and how you can increase your skills.

4. The Nature of Divine Calling

Divinely Appointed

Elders, though chosen by members of the local church, are called and appointed to their office by God. The form for the Ordination of Elders and Deacons (see *Psalter Hymnal*, pp. 1004-1006) repeatedly mentions this divine appointment, making reference to the three Persons of the Trinity:

The Father

▶ "God our heavenly Father, who has called you to these sacred offices. . . ."

▶ "Our merciful Father in heaven, we thank you that you have provided . . . elders."

The Son

▶ "As the Lord of the church he appoints leaders."

▶ "I charge you, people of God, to receive these officebearers as Christ's gift to the church."

The Holy Spirit

▶ "And by his Spirit equips them."

▶ "I charge you elders to 'guard yourselves and all the flock of which the Holy Spirit has made you overseers.'"

The form for the Ordination of Elders and Deacons drives the point home with this personal question: "Do you believe that in the call of this congregation God himself is calling you to these holy offices?" Synod 1987 underscored the importance of this call when it declared, "Officebearers are elected and called by the congregation, in which process those chosen must acknowledge the call of Jesus Christ" (*Acts of Synod 1987*, p. 393).

So as you perform your duties, remind yourself again and again of the reality that your mandate is from God!

Divine Backing

What are the practical implications of this divine appointment? You will not mysteriously find yourself endowed with all kinds of new gifts and skills. Your fellow members will not surround you with an extra measure of respect and awe. In fact, they may well oppose you in certain matters and may not always agree with your decisions. You may even find relationships with some parishioners strained.

But divine appointment will enable you to *deal confidently with unsettling doubts about your eldership.* If your appointment were only the outcome of the voting authority of the members, then your office would be no more than that of a member of a board. But because God himself has appointed you, you exercise your office in God's authority. You serve because God called you to serve. You still have your human limitations—you may not be the best speaker, you may be shy, you may be inept at times, you may make mistakes—but you must not entertain the defeatist notion "Others can do this better than I." You and God are in this assignment together!

Divine appointment has yet another aspect. When you are ordained to office, the minister addresses the congregation with these words: "I charge you, people of God, to receive these officebearers as Christ's gift to the church . . . . Hold them in honor; take their counsel seriously." Those are true and reassuring words. Both you and the congregation know that the office of elder is God-given and is, therefore, to be held in high regard.

Elders Who Govern

"Elders serve by governing in Christ's name. They received this task when Christ entrusted the apostles and their successors with the keys of the kingdom of heaven (Matt. 16:19). Elders are thus responsible for the spiritual well-being of God's people. They must provide true preaching and teaching, regular celebration of the sacraments, and faithful counsel and discipline . . . . And they must promote fellowship and hospitality among believers, ensure good order in the church, and stimulate witness to all people." —*Psalter Hymnal*, page 1004

"But we have this treasure in jars of clay to show that this all-surpassing power is from God and not from us."

—*2 Corinthians 4:7*

"Since we live by the Spirit, let us keep in step with the Spirit."

—*Galatians 5:25*

5. The Qualities of an Elder

The form for the Ordination of Elders and Deacons names a number of qualities or qualifications that should be embodied in all officebearers. While some may possess one of these more than others, and while no one fully displays all of them, still they describe the qualities expected in those who serve in church office.

- ▶ **Christlikeness.** You may not think of yourself as particularly Christlike, but all Christians are disciples of Jesus and called to become like him. Christlikeness is both a reality and an aspiration. It's a reality because we are baptized into Christ. Our baptism says we are united to Jesus Christ in his death and resurrection, and designated as sons and daughters of God in Christ. It's an aspiration because none of us are there yet. But even when we fail to be like the Master, we come to his cross for forgiveness and the renewing power of his Spirit.

- ▶ **Maturity in the faith.** A crop matures toward the end of a full season of growth. Similarly, elders must be "seasoned" in the faith. A mature faith involves both knowledge and action. It's a faith that knows and understands the basic truths of the Bible and the doctrines of the church. But mature faith also puts these truths into practice in everyday living. Marks of maturity are evident when as an elder you are able to discern biblical truth in complex and trying situations, reason with unreasonable people, and go for substance rather than show.

- ▶ **Prayer.** Prayer is the privilege and call of all believers, but it's especially necessary for elders. In prayer we express our true dependence on God, understanding that his gifts and blessing will only come to those who ask. A praying elder also models this quality to others in the ministries of visitation and discipling.

- ▶ **Patience.** This fruit of the Spirit does not come easily for most people. It clashes with our natural inclination to take action, and take it now. Patience is the slow-growing fruit of waiting with trust. The Latin word from which patience has been derived means "pain"; growing in patience usually comes through enduring painful and trying circumstances.

▶ **Humility.** Without humility, those given oversight can become overbearing. The word comes from a Latin word that means "to be close to the ground." You get the idea. Some of the people you serve have been beaten down by life. They are, as it were, lying on the ground. To truly serve them, you must get down on their level to make eye contact. Humility is the true spirit of leadership (Matt. 20:26-28).

The form also includes a prayer for two other important qualities: *enthusiasm* and *a sense of sustained awe.*

▶ **Enthusiasm** means "God-indwelled." By meditating on God's Word and allowing God to indwell us, we become "enthused" people. We also are God-indwelled because God is present in the church through the Holy Spirit. The indwelling of the Holy Spirit is God's greatest gift to us. The Spirit gives you, the officebearer, the power to express the gifts Christ has entrusted to you.

▶ **Awe** stems from a mixture of reverence, fear, and wonder. It's usually caused by something majestic and sublime. Awe and enthusiasm are closely related. Aren't those the feelings you get when you see the great works of God among his people? You can do the work of an elder more effectively when you practice that sense of awe. Without it the holy things of God tend to become commonplace. (For a study of other characteristics of elders, see Gal. 5:22-23; 1 Tim. 3:1-7; Titus 1:6-9; 1 Pet. 5:1-4.)

The form for the Ordination of Elders and Deacons mentions one more gift, seemingly in passing, in the charge to the elders. Elders are to be wise counselors. Wisdom is a quality so foundational that it deserves a section of its own in this book.

6. The Gift and Practice of Wisdom

Wisdom is a lamp that illumines all the other gifts God gives us. Some say that wisdom cannot be learned; you either have it or you don't. Some people never increase much in wisdom, even in old age. But anyone who earnestly desires to grow in wisdom will succeed.

Solomon prayed for wisdom and God granted his request (1 Kings 3:9-12). The apostle James advised all believers to ask God for wisdom (James 1:5) with the firm assurance that God will respond favorably to such prayers. And the exhortation to treasure wisdom is woven throughout the book of Proverbs. When the readers listen to the Word of the Lord and practice righteousness, they are wise. Wisdom is within reach of all those who listen to God speak. "Does not wisdom call out?" (Prov. 8:1).

A Special Kind of Seeing

Wisdom, at its root, comes from a Latin word meaning "to see." Seeing is a very important component of wisdom. You, the wise elder, carefully observe situations from all sides. You see them in their correct proportion. You see them in their relation to broader realities. You see their causal connections. You perceive the probable outcome of their interactions. You do all this intentionally. As you increase in wisdom, you become more adept at this approach. And as wisdom "grows on you," you will observe yourself as you truly are and you will practice wisdom unintentionally.

Wisdom enables you to understand your ideals, prejudices, hopes, memories, experiences, weaknesses, strengths, interests, misgivings, anger, and fears. When you come to terms with these inner realities, a greater degree of peace is within your reach. You will then understand how your inner life affects your relationships with people around you. Your parishioners, when you visit with them, will sense that you are transparent, that you seek their well-being from pure motives, and that you speak with honesty and impartiality.

A Special Kind of Doing

There are also some practices which, when consistently pursued, will gradually create a climate in which wisdom can grow and flourish.

Here are some examples:

- **Don't rush.** Give yourself some time before you make a decision or give advice in difficult situations. Sleep on it. Pray about it. Even then, if possible, live a few days with your intended advice or decision before you make it known.

- **Be comprehensive in your assessment of situations.** Have you considered all the facts? Do you understand the background of the events? Are you driven by a true desire to serve? Have you heard from all the parties involved? Have you sought good advice? Check your motives. Be a sympathetic player in the drama. Check your own fears. Acknowledge that it is sometimes hard to be totally honest with yourself.

- **Don't be a loner.** Wisdom flourishes best when counsel is taken communally. Seek the advice of your colleagues in office. Learn from them. Listen hard to those whose viewpoints differ from yours. Welcome and grow from encounters that stretch you.

- **Be a constructive ponderer.** It is not helpful to fret and worry about people and situations all day long. Rather, take some time out to concentrate intentionally on the matter at hand. Talk with yourself. Reason and argue with yourself. Keep at it! Make notes.

- **Weave prayer into such moments.** By doing so you will gain an accurate and helpful perspective on the situation you face. The course you choose will probably be illumined by wisdom.

- **Maintain your focus.** Church life can be confusing. As an elder you have a lot on your mind. Remind yourself to focus on the greater goal of church life. Focus on the ideals you have set for your work as an elder. Bring your inner resources to bear on the ultimate goal. The focused elder is likely to do his or her work with wisdom. (See also *Our World Belongs to God—A Contemporary Testimony*, paragraph 40; online at www.crcna.org.)

> "I keep asking that the God of our Lord Jesus Christ, the glorious Father, may give you the Spirit of wisdom. . . . I pray that the eyes of your heart may be enlightened."
>
> —Ephesians 1:17-18

7. Growing in Knowledge and Skills

It goes without saying that shepherding God's flock will require a good deal of your time. You should also expect to set aside time for training and study. Take advantage of opportunities to increase your knowledge and skill. In the long run you will be glad you did. By gaining knowledge and skill you will do a better job of serving the church. Here are some practical things you can do:

▶ Read the confessions of the church and the Church Order.

▶ Attend elders' conferences, Days of Encouragement, and workshops. They will prepare you for service and enrich you personally.

▶ If you are a new elder, make an appointment to sit down with an experienced elder and talk things over. You can learn a lot by doing so, and the fellowship will be valuable.

▶ Ask your council to set aside some time in the agenda for group study, selecting topics related to your work. Sometimes the pastor may take the initiative to arrange the discussion. Such study can contribute to the nurture of all officebearers. (For more on this, see *Guiding the Faith Journey*, Faith Alive Christian Resources, pp. 7-31.)

▶ Above all, return frequently to the Word of God!

8. Depending on the Bible

It's obvious, isn't it? All Christians should read the Bible, and elders should set the example. But you and I know from personal experience that it takes some doing to be a serious Bible reader.

The Rewards of Reading

Regular Bible reading brings two rewards to the elder. The form for the Ordination of Elders and Deacons hints at the first one: the Bible is the source from which you draw to minister to the people entrusted to your care. The form advises you to "know the Scriptures," which are "useful for teaching, rebuking, correcting, and training in righteousness" (2 Tim. 3:16). As you perform your tasks in the church, make mental notes of needs, challenges, problems, and struggles as you observe them. Then try to determine how the Bible addresses them.

The second benefit of Bible reading has to do with your own spiritual well-being. Life is demanding. Being an elder only adds to the stress. Be serious about recharging your spiritual batteries regularly. If you neglect your inner self, you will eventually "burn out." So make Bible reading a regular part of your daily routine.

Perhaps you will find it helpful to conclude your reading with a few moments of silence during which you ponder and pray over the verses you have just read. Then, throughout the day, intentionally try to recall the message that comes to you. It will help you to face the day in God's company and to discern God's will (see *Our World Belongs to God*, paragraphs 31-33).

Joining with other believers in a church-based Bible study group may also benefit you greatly. Such groups may be found in most churches. As an elder you will profit from either joining a study group or using your gift of leadership to start one.

Keys of the Kingdom

Your faithfulness to the Word of God has another implication.

In Matthew 16:18-19 we read a remarkable saying of Jesus. When Peter confesses the Savior's name, Jesus gives him a special promise: "And I tell you that you are Peter, and on this rock I will build my church, and the gates of death will

What a Privilege!

I have come to experience the work of an elder as a great privilege. There is really nothing that quite compares to it.
To help people spiritually, to encourage them to be strong and happy in the Lord, to share their joy of salvation, to know about their troubles and suffering, to travel with them in times of fear—these are blessed experiences that remain forever.

When I was a teenager, I would ask, "Dad, may I have the car tonight?" He would look thoughtful, then slowly hand over the keys. He didn't have to add many warnings. He knew that I understood it was a privilege, a trust, to hold those keys in my hands. Elders, in the service of Christ, hold keys in their hands—the keys of the kingdom!

Pastor John

not overcome it. I will give you the keys of the kingdom of heaven; whatever you bind on earth will be bound in heaven, and whatever you loose on earth will be loosed in heaven."

The churches of the Reformation have always held that the successors of the apostles are the officebearers appointed to the ministry of the Word and church discipline, for it was by the Word that Christ ordained to build the church (2 Cor. 5:19-21). "Elders serve by governing the church in Christ's name. They received this task when Christ entrusted the apostles and their successors with the keys of the kingdom of heaven. Elders are thus responsible for the spiritual well-being of God's people" (*Psalter Hymnal*, p. 1004).

You and your fellow officebearers have the power of the keys of the kingdom by virtue of being appointed to your office, conditioned by your faithfulness to the Scriptures and obedience to your Sender. You may assure those who believe with their heart and confess with their mouth that Jesus is Lord that they are part of the kingdom (Rom. 10:8-13). And you have the authority to announce to those who persist in stubborn disobedience that they have no part in the kingdom unless they repent. You will do that in close consultation with your fellow officebearers and according to the church's accepted protocol (see also section 50).

But to wield the keys of the kingdom also has a deeper, personal dimension. It means that you know you are sent and accompanied by the Savior and empowered by the Spirit. Whenever you think of the members of your district, whenever you serve them, be it ever so humbly, you serve with your Sender's permission.

9. Devoted to Prayer

Elders cannot serve well without regularly seeking the face of the great Shepherd. Yes, do it! Take time from your crowded schedule to pray.

First, pray for yourself. It will help you to deal with the busyness of your life. Prayer refreshes, replenishes, and strengthens the one who prays. As you exit your "prayer closet," you will do so with a new sense of wholeness and enthusiasm for your ministry.

In addition, pray for the individuals and families entrusted to your care. This is not optional. It is a requirement of the office you have accepted. The form for ordination affirms, "Officebearers must exercise their office with prayer." In the charge to the elders, you are directed to "pray continually for the church."

Here is an idea to make your prayers more meaningful. Consider making a list of people for whom you are responsible and adding details about their lives as you observe them. Then pray through the list at regular intervals. You will soon find that such prayer is a worthy component of your activities. You will probably also find that prayer will help you to fight against procrastination. And yes, do place your own name on your prayer list too!

Power of Prayer

"Prayer is not overcoming God's reluctance. It is laying hold of God's highest willingness."

—*Richard Trench*

A Prayer for Elders

Grant them the gift of your Holy Spirit, that their hearts may be set on fire with love for you and those committed to their care. Make them pure in heart as those who have the mind of Christ. Give them vision to discern your purposes for the church and the world you love. Keep them faithful to the end in all their service, that when the chief Shepherd appears, they may receive glory, a crown that never fades.

—*Book of Common Order of the Church of Scotland*

10. Managing Your Time

How can you do it all? Time is like water—it can disappear ever so slowly. However, time, like water, can be managed. Time management can be learned; you can even make it a way of life.

An elder with whom I once served stopped by my study to tell me that he had not visited the people in his district that season. He explained that he had just been too busy. It seemed to weigh heavily on him. Then I asked him whether he did any planning and scheduling in his life. "Not really," he said. So I made a proposal: "Would you be able to devote one evening every two weeks to visiting?" He thought for a moment and nodded. "Now suppose that of the twelve months of the year you would designate eight months for visiting," I said. "Fair enough," he replied. I added, "That would give you sixteen evenings during that eight-month season. Suppose you would schedule two visits per evening. That would enable you to make thirty-two visits." "Amazing," he said. "That's more than the twenty-five addresses in my district."

Districts as Small Communities of Members

Although in this book I refer to *districts*, your church may use a different system of organizing members of the congregation into care groups. What I mean is the group of people who are entrusted to your care.

Controlling the calendar is, however, only half the battle. Other steps are involved. You may wish to begin by making a survey of your tasks. Settle for what you can do, and then set goals accordingly. Only then can you do your scheduling. Lay out the weeks and months of the church year in blocks on large sheets of paper. Pencil in the stated meetings of the council, consistory, and committees. Next, mark the times you want to set aside for visiting. Make appointments well ahead of time. Keep track of tasks performed and visits made.

I suggest that you discuss this process with your spouse. Mutual agreement on the extent of your involvement is important. If, in the course of the season, you are away from home more than you and your spouse had anticipated, you should review your schedule and make adjustments.

Of course, circumstances are unpredictable and unforeseen events may wreak havoc with your schedule. Don't worry; you can always revise. Let your colleagues know when there are tasks you simply cannot complete. Perhaps they can help. As you deal with unexpected timing conflicts, *remember that you would be worse off with no planning and no scheduling.* Now you have a means to track and reschedule tasks you could not do. That's one of the advantages of planning: it helps you practice good stewardship of your time.

11. Feeling Inadequate

All elders feel inadequate at times—and you will too. There are no simple solutions. Serving the Master doesn't happen without pain and struggle. But remember that "those who sow with tears will reap with songs of joy" (Ps. 126:5). When you find yourself caught in times of doubt, consider these suggestions:

▶ Make sure that you have the right perspective on your role as an elder. You have accepted the responsibility of ministering to God's people, and you will want to do that in a spirit of involvement and empathy. But you are not responsible for the outcome. You minister on Christ's behalf. God guides the results—in his time and in his way. So don't berate yourself for the seeming absence of success.

▶ Don't belittle yourself if your work seems to flounder. Your office carries dignity and honor (Church Order, Art. 2). That may not seem very real to you, but to Christ it is. Even if the members of your district only infrequently express their appreciation in some meaningful way, you can carry on with the confidence that your congregation will keep the promise it made when you were installed to "hold [you] in honor . . . [and to] sustain [you] in prayer and encourage [you] . . . especially when [you] feel the burden of [your] office."

▶ The ordination form includes another wonderful promise: "[The Lord] appoints leaders and by his Spirit equips them . . . ." Remember—when you do the best you can, the Spirit will give the increase. God's invisible blessings are often the most enduring ones! Don't neglect to seek out your colleagues in ministry for mutual prayer, consultation, encouragement, and thanksgiving. You can be one another's greatest encouragers (see also section 48).

12. A Spiritual Vision for the Church

All believers are called to the ministry of reconciliation, says the apostle Paul. "We are therefore Christ's ambassadors, as though God were making his appeal through us. We implore you on Christ's behalf: Be reconciled to God" (2 Cor. 5:20).

This is Paul's spiritual vision for the church. You stand in a great apostolic tradition as you lead your congregation toward the same vision. So pray that the people under your care will experience reconciliation with God and with each other.

The church has a spiritual purpose that is invisible to the world. It may not always be as visible as you had hoped. But remind yourself over and over that the ministry of reconciliation is the foundation of your congregation's ministry. Collectively as elders and deacons, deepen in the awareness that the entire church program should be slanted toward the reconciliation God desires. This ministry of reconciliation stretches way beyond the church to the world—in fact, the church exists to bring that message and example of reconciliation to the world.

> **The Least**
>
> "No one wanted to be considered least. Then Jesus took a towel and a basin and so redefined greatness."
>
> —Richard Foster, *Celebration of Discipline*

The form for ordination includes this prayer: "Under [these officebearers'] guidance may your church grow in every spiritual grace, in faith which is open and unashamed. . . ." Keep that vision! Maintain that focus! (See also section 53.)

Moving among God's People

We now turn our attention to the personal contact you will have with the people under your care. This activity must be viewed in the context of your work as a member of consistory and council. These two areas are closely connected. When you minister to people, you do so as a consistory member. And, conversely, the work of your consistory and council must always display a deep concern for the welfare of your people.

So while we distinguish between the tasks of personal caregiving and participation in the work of consistory and council, we don't separate them.

Note: In keeping with synodical usage, we refer to *consistory* as the body of elders and minister(s) and to *council* as the body of deacons, elders, and minister(s).

13. Districts

The members of most congregations are organized into districts. (For the purpose of this book, *district* means the specific portion of the congregation under each elder's care.) Having your own district enables you to develop a personal relationship with a limited number of parishioners. Most congregations elect elders and deacons for a term of three years. That has been widely found to be about the right length of time. Ideally, each elder stays with the same district for the entire three years. From the beginning, you'll want to be intentionally aware that you are accompanying your people on their faith journey of life. You'll get to know them, share their sorrows and joys, and witness their struggles toward growth.

Having a district for that length of time enables you to bring continuity and consistency to your ministry. Every contact builds on the previous one. You develop mutual trust—one great prerequisite for doing your work effectively.

Some churches have large districts, each served by a team of two elders. Others have smaller districts with one elder in charge. Both have advantages. When you are part of a team, you and your fellow elders can encourage and advise each other. When difficulties develop, you can deliberate together. Between the two of you, accountability will probably develop. It's also helpful in some cases to make visits together.

If you serve a district alone, you have fewer people to oversee. You may get to know them better, and it takes less time to make the rounds.

In many congregations a deacon is assigned to each district. This is a commendable arrangement. The district elder and district deacon can function as a team with the understanding that each does the work appropriate to his or her office. They keep each other informed about needs and opportunities they observe. They may plan activities together and make visits together when that seems best.

Many churches cluster membership activities around the districts, generally with good results. If this describes your church, you may consider appointing a district coordinator to facilitate activities. The elder, deacon, and coordinator may form a team to organize events and administer district life.

In some churches elder care districts are arranged geographically. This enhances ministry to a certain area of the community, fosters interaction and care between members who live close to each other, and stimulates witness to neighbors.

Many churches encourage members to participate in small groups. In such groups a dozen (or fewer) members meet at regular times to pray, meditate, study, and share mutual concerns. District elders should remain in regular contact with the groups in their districts and visit them as time permits. Small group leaders may be drawn into the district leadership. (See also *Guiding the Faith Journey*, Faith Alive Christian Resources, pp. 53-58.)

14. Getting to Know Your People

In order to be a spiritual blessing to the people you serve, you must become acquainted with them. Life for the people you serve may be a difficult saga in which successes and setbacks are constantly absorbing their attention. When they have particular problems and personal pain, they will appreciate your concern and empathy. In times of good fortune, they will appreciate your interest.

Reaching Out

There probably are more lonely people in your district than you had imagined. Through your good care they will experience the community of believers. This is especially true of the elderly. When your congregation gathers for fellowship activities, seek out individual members and discreetly inquire about ongoing developments in their lives. They will deeply appreciate your intelligent concern.

Children and young people need your special attention. Their lives are filled with excitement but also with anxiety. Ordinarily you will need to initiate contact with them. They may not give their trust readily, but if you show consistent, genuine interest in their well-being they will open their hearts to you.

Understanding People

The right perspective opens the way toward the right service. Try to size up people and situations correctly. Jesus was able to fulfill the task God gave him because he saw everything in the right perspective. So his followers can serve best when they have "the mind of Christ" (1 Cor. 2:16)—Christ's perspective on people and situations.

Christ's Vision of the Church

Christ saw the multitude not as a hostile crowd, but as sheep without a shepherd (Matt. 9:36); he saw prodigals not as hopeless cases, but as children whom the Father would welcome home (Luke 15:11-32); he saw outsiders not as people who don't count for much, but as potential Good Samaritans (Luke 10:25-37); he saw the church not as a body that is constantly failing, but as his beautiful bride (Rev. 22:17), as the salt of the earth (Matt. 5:13), and as the light of the world (Matt. 5:14).

How One Elder Kept in Touch with His Care District

As soon as he had been appointed an elder and assigned to a district, Matthew sent a general letter to the members telling them of his readiness to serve them. Before and after church he made a point of seeking them out and chatting briefly. He memorized the names of the children and greeted them whenever he saw them at church. He made a list of members' birthdates and sent cards or e-mails. Whenever he spotted one of his people in the hardware store or the grocery store, he greeted him or her warmly. Periodically he organized a district get-together for the members to meet each other. After a while, Matthew found that the people in his district began to contact him when they were sick or had other needs.

15. Record Keeping

Your Logbook

Record keeping is of vital importance in your work as an elder. As soon as you are installed in office, set up a personal logbook on your computer or in a notebook. Write in it all the basic information for every member in your district: address, phone number, age, job, school, skills and gifts, functions in church and beyond, and so on. In the months ahead, remember to record important events in the members' lives, note when you visit them, and jot down any highlights. Review your logbook regularly to remain current with the members of your district. Once your people know that you are sincerely interested in them, they will come to trust you and will be more likely to contact you when needs arise.

My logbook frequently reminded me of an overdue visit or a phone call I should make. I found that record keeping does not take much time, and it gave me ongoing assurance that I was on top of things pastorally. I made it a practice to regularly page though my logbook, which often set me to praying for the people I had come to love. It was as if my soul visited them briefly.

At the end of your term as an elder, consider making a summary of your log for the benefit of your successor, being careful to omit confidential information.

Your Church's Administrative System

Your council should see to it that your congregation benefits from a well-kept administrative system. Minutes of council meetings, committee meetings, and task force meetings must be kept in good form and carefully recorded. Financial dealings and membership changes should be recorded meticulously. (See Church Order, Art. 68.)

My Logbook

The logbook I kept as an elder included entries like these:

- John B.: laid off; visited March 3

- Mary O.: valedictorian, high school graduation

- Beth and Mike K.: baby boy John Adam, Nov. 2

- Bert P.: left for University of New Mexico

- Gert A.: transferred to Room 166 at the Manor; Apr.

- Jane E.: would like to play violin in church; told the committee, Apr. 3

- Claude VB.: bought new truck

- Paul U.: became partner in firm

- Helen and Pete DV.: baby remains colicky; phoned Oct. 10

- John B.: job prospects still bleak; phoned March 30

- David and Sally L.: 50th wedding anniversary; visited Sept. 13

- Mary V.: will be 10 next Sunday

- Pat and John C.: kitchen fire, July 18

- Jack T.: father in Canada died, June 2

- Debra S.: discussed problem she had with music committee, Feb. 11

- Gert A.: visited April 4

- Beth K.: phoned; discussed details of baptism, young John

- John B.: phoned about employment, Apr. 23

16. Forming a Spiritual Community

In Reformed churches we emphasize God's covenant relationship to us and our covenant relationships to each other. In covenant love, God solemnly commits himself to be our God. God also calls us into covenant relationships with each other. Thus we are not merely members of a voluntary society, but committed by covenant to God and to each other.

A Dual Covenant Relationship

The spiritual life of your congregation therefore has two dimensions. The people grow in their relationship to God *and* to each other. Through the church's ministry the members increasingly experience the reality of covenantal life: love for God and for their neighbor (Mark 12:30-31).

This dual covenantal vision should mark your service to God's people. This does not suggest that you should always engage in "spiritual talk" when you meet a member of your district. Take advantage of small talk with your parishioners, but always keep their need for spiritual growth in mind. The apostle Paul said, "We will in all things grow up into him who is the head, that is, Christ" (Eph. 4:15).

That same covenantal concern helps you see every believer as part of the Christian community. It hurts an elder's heart when members don't feel at home in the congregation, when they feel slighted, or when they are divided over issues and policies. People treasure fellowship, a sense of belonging; the absence of such fellowship is the most common reason why people leave.

Paul follows his words about growing into Christ by describing this sequence: "From him the whole body, joined and held together by every supporting ligament, grows and builds itself up in love, as each part does its work" (Eph. 4:16). Elders become increasingly *covenant minded*: establishing people in God and establishing people in community. They have heard the apostle Peter's challenge: "To the elders among you, I appeal as a fellow elder. . . . Be shepherds of God's flock that is under your care, watching over them, . . . being examples to the flock" (1 Pet. 5:1-3).

Nurturing Relationships

Spiritual development has an additional dimension. Note that Paul teaches that the body "grows and builds itself up in love, as each part does its work." A spiritual community experiences well-being when the members care for each other. Actually that's how most pastoral work is done in flourishing churches: members pastor members. Mutual giving and receiving of care becomes a way of life for the congregation. (See *Our World Belongs to God*, paragraph 39, and *Guiding the Faith Journey*, pp. 65-95, Faith Alive Christian Resources.)

The apostle John summarizes such spiritual growth: "Love one another. . . . We know that we have passed from death to life, because we love each other. . . . This is how we know what love is: Jesus Christ laid down his life for us. And we ought to lay down our lives for one another. If any one of you has material possessions and sees a brother or sister in need but has no pity on them, how can the love of God be in you? Dear children, let us not love with words or tongue but with actions and in truth" (1 John 3:11, 14, 16-18). (Note that the word *truth* is related to "troth" and "trust," both key elements in wholesome relationships.)

This kind of spiritual growth is emphasized in the Church Order: "The consistory shall . . . foster a spirit of love and openness within the fellowship" (Art. 79b).

Promoting Mutually Nurturing Relationships

▶ In your contacts with your district members, discern whether each person has at least one enriching relationship with another member. Challenge members to encourage and help each other. Perhaps you can ask one member to visit another member who is ill. Or you can direct one member toward another member who has a specific need, such as bringing a meal to someone who is ill. Elders, deacons, and ministers may need to cooperate in making these arrangements.

▶ In your district's group activities, take the opportunity to remind members of the need for mutual care. Invite participants to express prayer concerns and challenge them to pray for specific needs.

Prayer Chain

Prayer chains (phone or e-mail) function best if people are trained to keep their conversation brief and to the point, simply relaying the message. This prevents rumor and misinformation and focuses the chain on the ministry of prayer.

▶ Most churches now have a telephone or e-mail prayer chain to inform members of needs, joys, sicknesses, events, and challenges. Sharing items of communal interest contributes to a sense of intimacy. Your district will benefit from its own prayer chain, especially if you facilitate its smooth functioning.

▶ Churches often publish congregational newsletters and distribute lists of prayer concerns. Encourage your members to use these vehicles to make news and prayer items known to the larger church body.

▶ Pay close attention to new members, seekers, and inquirers, many of whom may struggle with loneliness and other difficulties. By establishing a relationship of trust with them, you may be able to link them up with caring members of your district.

▶ Tell your pastor that you would like to assist in establishing nurturing relationships in the church. Encourage your pastor to make this type of spiritual development part of his Word ministry.

17. Spiritual Formation

Assurance and Doubt

You will find that many of your members have two basic concerns:

- ▶ How to experience and live out their salvation.

- ▶ How to deal with nagging doubt and failures.

Recognize that these are two sides of one coin. The people in your care yearn to live close to God, yet they are often disappointed in themselves. Life comes with so many demands and pressures. They want to experience joy, but they often feel empty and sad. The term *spiritual formation* is often used for ministry that helps people in their pursuit of spiritual health. That is where much of your work is focused.

Grace and Spiritual Formation

Spiritual formation is Paul's way of talking about becoming like Christ. He says to the Galatians that he is in the spiritual pain of childbirth "until Christ is formed in you" (Gal. 4:19). In the gospels, spiritual formation means becoming disciples of Jesus—people who follow him and become like him. The major task of the church, according to Jesus, is to "make disciples" (Matt. 28:19). And that's the elder's main task as well.

But spiritual formation and discipleship are not primarily what we do by our own effort to become pleasing to God. Because of Christ's death and resurrection, God justified us and declared us to be his children (Rom. 5:1-11; 1 John 3:1). We are saved by faith in Christ. And Christ empowers our formation into his likeness by the Spirit (that's why it's called *spiritual* formation). Our certainty, our hope, our foundation is always Christ, who by his grace saves us and brings us to mature faith. You will help your people to look upon Christ. Placing our trust in personal piety and banking on it for certainty means we are in for disappointment and frustration.

Throughout history there have been movements that spelled out rigid patterns of piety. This established code of conduct was the condition for belonging to the community. The members showed loyalty to the community, spoke its language, and defended its positions on issues. The community, in turn, afforded the members a sense of belonging, security, self-worth, and, especially, assurance of salvation. Legalism and bondage invariably followed in the wake of such developments.

In your ministry to God's people, assure them of the great truth of *salvation by grace* through faith in Christ. In Christ, believers experience the power of the Holy Spirit, through which they serve their Savior and Lord. As an elder, you are part of the Word ministry that establishes the members more firmly in their Savior.

At the same time, we all need to grow up into Christ. The classic spiritual disciplines of prayer, Bible reading, worship, community, and so on, are practices that shape us into Christ's likeness. They require effort and some self-discipline, but they are not heavy burdens or even laws we lay on people. When people begin to grow in Christ, they want to grow more, and you will find that they seek out these disciplines in the pursuit of spiritual growth.

You will find wonderful summaries of the Word in the confessions of the church. (Look in the back of the *Psalter Hymnal* or visit www.crcna.org and click on "Beliefs.") The Heidelberg Catechism, for example, explains the Apostles' Creed (Lord's Days 8-23). This is splendid teaching material, and it is also suitable for group discussion.

Note also these wonderful statements in Lord's Day 32 of the catechism (Q&A 86):

▶ "We have been delivered from our misery by God's grace alone through Christ."

▶ "To be sure, Christ has redeemed us by his blood."

▶ "But we do good because Christ by his Spirit is also renewing us to be like himself."

▶ "We do good so that we may be assured of our faith by its fruits."

▶ " . . . so that by our godly living our neighbors may be won over to Christ."

Spiritual formation needs a firm biblical foundation and perspective. Once this is a growing concern among your people, they will be motivated to seek spiritual nurture and discipline: reading Scripture, meditating on Scripture, praying alone and together, talking with God, setting aside time for devotional reading, and participating in retreats and conferences.

Study Sources

Check out the following resources for helping people grow in their faith:

- *Guiding the Faith Journey*, Neil de Koning, Faith Alive Christian Resources, 1996

- *Disciples* series, Year 2; Faith Alive Christian Resources

- *Keys to a Praying Church*, Alvin Vander Griend, Faith Alive Christian Resources, 1996

- *Space for God*, Don Postema, Faith Alive Christian Resources, 1983, 1997

- *Speaking of God,* Ben Campbell Johnson, John Knox, 1991, pages 11-30

- *Today—The Family Altar*, booklet for daily meditations, Back to God Ministries International

18. Stewardship

Those who walk in the power of God's grace dedicate their lives to God's service. *They live a life of stewardship.* Stewardship springs from the vision that God made us, redeemed us, and provides for us; what we are and what we have we owe to God. In stewardship we dedicate ourselves and our possessions to God.

What Does Stewardship Mean in Practice?

Consider the Macedonian Christians. "We want you to know about the grace that God has given the Macedonian churches," says the apostle Paul. "In the midst of a very severe trial, their overflowing joy and their extreme poverty welled up in rich generosity. For I testify that they gave as much as they were able, and even beyond their ability. Entirely on their own, they urgently pleaded with us for the privilege of sharing in this service to the Lord's people" (2 Cor. 8:1-4).

Stewardship had become a way of life for the Macedonian Christians despite their "extreme poverty." We follow their example, for we know that God is the owner of our skills, our ambitions, our things, and our many loves. What we own is simply on loan from God. We manage our lives for him. We are his *stewards*.

Stewards are secure people. They know that God is always there. And so they go in his name to the poor who need relief, to the grieving who need solace, to the hungry who need bread, to the lonely who need a friend. They are there when the church needs workers, when campaigns need funds, and when programs need volunteers. Stewardship is a way of life.

What Can You Do to Promote Stewardship?

Practice financial stewardship in your own life. Manage your affairs wisely and responsibly. Be generous in supporting God's work in the world. Make stewardship a spiritual service for yourself. Only then will you have the spiritual courage and freedom to lead your members in their stewardly calling.

Set forth a clear vision of biblical stewardship in council meetings, with your pastor, and among your members. Stewardship goes far beyond fundraising. It includes everything from the care of our property to the type of coffee cups we use. Its first beneficiary is the giver, as he or she actively shares in the coming of God's kingdom on earth. What your members give is determined more by their motivation for giving than by the extent of their resources. (For other helpful suggestions, see *Firstfruits: A Stewardship Guide for Church Leaders*, Faith Alive Christian Resources.)

In our busy culture, time is at a premium. One of the most important areas of stewardship, then, is how we manage our time. Encourage the people in your care to spend time in the spiritual disciplines of prayer and Bible reading and to offer their time in service to others as opportunities arise in their church and in their neighborhoods.

First Church's Financial Struggles

The elders, deacons, and pastor of First Church met with the finance committee to discuss money matters. "We are not meeting this year's budget—not by a long shot," said the spokesperson for the committee. "The projected deficit runs into the thousands."

Next came the deacons' report. The secretary handed out sheets containing a long list of causes for which the deacons proposed support. The deacons explained that the total of their proposed annual giving to various causes was higher than ever due to increased needs everywhere.

Discussion followed.

Then a deacon said, "Our congregation is not rich, but it is not poor either, and our members are not stingy. Last month we had a special offering for Mrs. K's eye surgery, and we collected twice the amount needed. I propose that we tell the congregation about our dilemma, that money is needed for our vibrant ministry program, but also for the indispensable ministries of these causes. And let us trust that the congregation will respond."

The following Sunday a deacon explained the challenge to the congregation, and the minister shared his vision of stewardship. Later that year a grateful finance committee reported that the budget had been met, and the deacons noted that they had received sufficient funds to cover checks sent to every special cause.

19. In the World

No one can fully understand the dynamics of being *in the world* but not *of the world*. Be aware that society affects your people in at least two ways:

- ▶ It entices them with material rewards.

- ▶ It frightens them with threats of evil and doom.

The realities of the modern world especially challenge the church's ministry in two ways as well.

First, the church must be *prophetically faithful*. It must seek to instill in its members a deep sensitivity toward holy living. It must be God's voice in society, calling the ruling authorities to champion goodness, decency, justice, and righteousness. Jesus said to his Father in heaven, "I have given them your word and the world has hated them, for they are not of the world any more than I am of the world. My prayer is not that you take them out of the world but that you protect them from the evil one. They are not of the world, even as I am not of it. Sanctify them by the truth; your word is truth" (John 17:14-17).

Second, the church must focus on the ministry of *consolation and mercy*. Fear is becoming all-pervasive; people increasingly see their church as a haven of safety and protection. Overcome by loneliness, they look to their church to find genuine fellowship.

So how can you be equipped to meet such awesome challenges?

- ▶ Never underestimate the power of prayer. Great revivals have always resulted from believers joining in prayer. And those revivals have often been God's means of transforming societies and restoring a measure of well-being to the nations.

- ▶ Officebearers must see to it that the local church's ministry has a dual focus: the well-being of its members and outreach to the world. Evangelism, the practice of mercy, and the kingdom pursuit of justice are as important as pastoral care for church members.

▶ Churches everywhere are discovering the blessings of being involved in a variety of projects aimed at alleviating suffering, poverty, and distress. Young people, adults, and retirees are going to depressed areas at home and abroad to repair homes, clean up after disasters, and build schools, churches, and medical clinics. Christian Reformed people are working to advance causes of justice and mercy in Canada and the United States. Members come together to discuss how they can best sound a Christian testimony in their workplace. As an elder, be sure to support such important initiatives!

Remember to keep the vision alive: In the world but not of the world, and yes, *for the world*.

Hope for the World

Still, despair and rebellious pride fill the earth:
Some, crushed by failure
or broken by pain,
give up on life and hope and God.
Others, shaken,
but still hoping for human triumph,
work feverishly to realize their dreams.
As believers in God,
we also struggle with the spirits of this age,
resisting them in the power of the Spirit,
testing them by God's sure Word.

—*Our World Belongs to God*, paragraph 3

In the World

"I simply argue that the cross be raised again at the center of the marketplace as well as on the steeple of the church. I am recovering the claim that Jesus was not crucified in a cathedral between two candles, but on a cross between two thieves, on the town garbage heap, at a crossroad so cosmopolitan they had to write his title in Hebrew, Latin, and Greek. It was the kind of place where cynics talk smut, thieves curse, and soldiers gamble. That's where he died. And that's where Christians ought to be."

—*George MacLeod*

20. Making a Visit

Looking back at the time-honored custom of annual visits, we may remember some of them as being a bit stilted and officious. But the tradition has ancient roots. Paul visited believers from house to house (Acts 20:20), and churches that practice regular pastoral visits are the richer for it.

Different Kinds of Visits

There was a time when Christian Reformed churches thought of their membership as predominantly composed of families. So we spoke of *family visitation*. Today many churches count more single people than families among their members. The Church Order uses the designation *home visit* (Art. 65), but that term does not cover all situations either. Today's elders are just as likely to visit their people in a room at church or in a restaurant over coffee.

In the following sections we consider different kinds of visits: to married couples, to parents and children, to single members, to the elderly, to young people, to those who are ill or who struggle with disabilities or addiction, and so on.

Frequency and Motivation

Church Order Article 65 (referred to above) stipulates that an "annual home visitation" be made, but in many churches such visits are made less frequently. There are at least two reasons for this.

First, the individualism of society increasingly infiltrates the life of the church. As a result some members are reluctant to welcome in-home visits, and those who are unfamiliar with the tradition may find it strange or even invasive. People may even think (though they're not likely to say it), *What business is it of yours to ask about my spiritual welfare?* In these cases, a visit outside the home may be best, and the emphasis of the visit should be on support and friendship.

Second, we live in demanding times. Elders and parishioners have limited discretionary time. Some consistories have adopted the practice of asking elders to make a commitment as to how often they will visit the members in their care during their term of office. This may be helpful in motivating you to keep closer contact with your people.

Your motivation will also be strengthened by focusing on the purpose of these visits: to encourage, strengthen, and affirm your members in their personal relationship to their Savior (Eph. 3:14-21; 4:11-16).

You can do that by centering the discussion on such matters as an individual's commitment to the Lord, the assurance of salvation, the expression of faith in daily life, relationships of Christian love, and so on.

You come as a representative of your Sender, Christ himself. So lay aside all trepidation and fear. You do not lean on your knowledge or your "people skills"; you come armed with the gospel and a sincere desire to help people become more firmly grounded in their faith.

The Visit

Here are some suggestions on how to call on a family—a husband and a wife, and perhaps some children, or a single parent with children.

A Perspective

The heart of a church's ministry is the preaching of the Word of God in worship services. The Word comes to the congregation collectively. All those present hear the same Word of life. Inasmuch as the minister is faithful to the Bible, he or she speaks with authority.

A parallel situation prevails when elders visit individual members. The Word is now centered on just one person's (or one couple's) faith walk. Elders seek to bring the Word to bear on that member's individual needs and his or her walk with Christ. When elders are faithful to the Word of God, they minister in the authority of Christ. Through those visits the church reaches out into an individual's life.

Schedule the visit well ahead of time (as a rule of thumb, it's good to schedule two visits per evening). As you approach the house, pause a moment and clear your mind. Do you feel relaxed and positive about this visit? Ask God to bless it.

As you are seated, remind yourself to pay attention to the family members. Express your appreciation to your host(s) for receiving you.

The visit now begins. It is important to be gracious, but also to keep pleasantries to a minimum. It is very easy to be drawn into small talk that can sidetrack the visit unnecessarily. Remind yourself that your prime concern is to learn how these people are doing in their walk with God.

The Three-Step Model

1. Listen attentively. Your foremost concern is this family's well-being in the Lord. So begin with a very simple question that most people can relate to:

How are you doing? People like to express their concerns. They appreciate a sympathetic, trusted listener. Pay careful attention. Then broaden that question a bit. How are they doing health-wise? In their daily work? Their relationships? Family matters? What might be their worries? Joys? Allow them to explain. These things are important to people. Enter thoughtfully into their story. Have you sensed the weight of what they tell you? It's far more important that you listen attentively and sympathetically than that you offer advice.

2. Solicit an emotional response. Do this by asking questions like these:

▶ Were you afraid when you had to make that decision?

▶ Were you relieved when you got that news?

▶ Are you still worried?

▶ Do you find it hard to forgive that person?

▶ Do you lie awake at night thinking about this problem?

▶ Do you find it hard to pray about that?

▶ Does this affect your relationship to Christ?

Such questions may serve as catalysts for people to come to terms with their feelings and then express them. Pay careful attention. Don't interrupt. Don't change the topic quickly.

3. Bring God into the picture. Do it modestly, gently, kindly, naturally, but without excuses. Don't be judgmental. Assure people of God's grace and of his love for those who are burdened. Where there is an apparent need for God's forgiveness, give assurance that God is eager to forgive upon confession. God is an accepting, heavenly Father. Remind people of God's promises. But remain the listener; your listening affirms people.

Further Help

Most elders will testify that visits often turn out differently than they had planned or hoped. The three-step approach may not always work. If that's the case, you may want to engage the family in a more general discussion about their relationship to the Lord. You may want to raise some of the following questions:

- How do you feel assured of salvation?

- How have you experienced the forgiveness of sin?

- Do the members of your family discuss their spiritual experiences together?

- What pattern do you use in reading the Bible?

- In what ways are you blessed in your prayer life?

- In what specific ways do you serve the Savior?

- Do your family members relate well to each other?

- In what ways do cultural pressures (such as media, busyness, or work) impact your family's ability to follow Jesus?

What to Listen For

- As you listen attentively, you may sense some underlying concerns. Are people hesitant to talk about something? Be discreet, but probe gently. Assure them that if they would like to discuss a certain matter in more detail later, you will be happy to make a follow-up call.

- Be sure to guide the discussion. Don't let it stray from the purpose of your visit. Keep your focus on the relationship of this family to the Lord and how that works out in their daily lives. Avoid advising. Don't talk about yourself.

- Don't overstay your welcome. The visit should last no more than an hour. If you avoid small talk and ask questions connected with your mission, you can cover a lot of ground in less than one hour. Again, when difficult problems surface, schedule a follow-up visit.

- Most people will appreciate your reading an appropriate Bible passage. Before the home visit season begins, make a list of suitable passages. If possible, select one that has been dealt with in a recent sermon or Bible study to connect the visit with the life of the larger congregation. Keep the passage fairly short.

- A brief closing prayer is generally fitting. Ask what they would like to have you pray for. The prayer should be marked by a loving concern for the family, and should include items that were part of your discussion.

Children at the Lord's Supper

Should children be present at the visit? Yes, by all means. You may wish to suggest that they be present when you schedule the visit with their parents. It is edifying for children to hear their parents' personal testimony. Tactfully draw the children into the discussion. Ask them about their lives and their love of Jesus.

On the other hand, the presence of children, while in itself delightful, may also limit the scope and honest exchange of the visit. If you know that there will be serious matters to discuss or are aware of challenging issues within the family, it may be wise to arrange the visit without children present, or at least ask to speak with the parents alone at some point.

What to Avoid

▶ Don't argue. In case of disagreement, state your conviction briefly or speak a word of Christian testimony without becoming defensive. *It's especially important not to get drawn into a matter over which there is open congregational disagreement.* If the consistory has decided a matter, whether or not you personally agree, it's your responsibility to listen carefully, explain the consistory's decision as clearly and persuasively as possible, and acknowledge that there can be honest but loving disagreement.

▶ Don't be a problem solver. People will tell you of hardships if they feel you're a sympathetic listener. Affirm them by speaking words of empathy and encouragement; assure them of God's nearness. This will allow them to experience that they belong to the Christian community.

▶ Don't solicit criticism of church practices, policies, or the pastor. Your visit focuses on the relationship of this family to God. Should criticisms come, assure people that the council is always willing to receive their suggestions and questions regarding the church's programs and practices. Should they express deep misgivings, make a follow-up call. Be aware that some people may attempt to get an elder to agree with them in order to gather a growing movement of discontent.

▶ Don't get bogged down in a discussion of issues—there are better forums for members and officebearers to dialogue about issues. But don't shy away from discussing disagreeable subjects as long as they have to do with the family's walk with the Lord. If the problems you encounter appear to be too complex, seek the help of the pastor or others with special competence.

▶ Don't attempt to fill every moment of silence after you have spoken, even if the silences make you uncomfortable. Show people respect by giving them time to respond.

- Avoid questions that can be answered by yes or no—this tends to shut conversation down.

- Again, remember that your task is to be an attentive listener. Don't lose focus of that goal.

Reporting to the Consistory

What people say during your visit should remain between them and you. It should not be shared with others. People assume they are talking with you in confidence; don't break that trust.

Should the people you're visiting alert you to a trend in congregational life or express a concern about some church matter, ask if they want you to report their concern to the council or consistory. If they agree, be sure to inform them at a later date of the council's response. (See also section 45.)

When a visit turns out well, you may report your positive evaluation to the consistory as a matter of thanksgiving. When a visit turns out badly, you may express your concern to the consistory, without mentioning details, as a matter for intercessory prayer.

After a season of home visits and appropriate feedback, elders are in a better position to assess the spiritual health of the congregation and to devise a program of effective pastoral care.

For other helpful material see *Guiding the Faith Journey*, pages 21-24, 59-63, 101-107 and *So You've Been Asked to Make Visits*, both from Faith Alive Christian Resources.

An Elder's First Visit

Joel had just been elected as elder and was about to make his first family visit. He approached the visit with some fear. Fortunately he was teamed up with an older elder who had served several terms.

Joel said to his teammate, "To be honest, I find it very hard to talk about spiritual things. I am not looking forward to this visit." His older colleague said, "I know what you mean, but remember that God is part of everyday life."

As the visit began, the older elder asked the husband about his work. The husband answered that his company had been laying people off and that he was not sure whether his job was secure. The older elder spoke words of empathy and understanding. He then asked the husband if he had been able to pray about these painful realities, and whether he had been able to put his trust in the Lord now that the future was so uncertain. He also asked the wife if she had found it possible to encourage her husband and whether she had been able to place her trust in her God.

Joel listened to this conversation with deep respect. He realized that these parents and the older elder were discussing their relationship to the Lord in a way that was totally genuine and devoid of artificiality.

Suggested Readings for Pastoral Visits

Saved by grace
Romans 5:1-11
Romans 7:14-25
Romans 8:1-8
Ephesians 1:3-10
Ephesians 2:1-10

Forgiveness and blessings
Psalm 32:1-7
Psalm 51:1-13
Psalm 130
Isaiah 40:1-8
Isaiah 53:1-9
Luke 15:11-24

God helps his people
Psalm 46
Psalm 91:1-8
Psalm 108:1-6
Psalm 121
Psalm 145:8-21
Isaiah 40:9-17
Isaiah 40:21-26
Matthew 6:25-34
Matthew 7:7-14
Luke 12:22-31
Ephesians 3:14-21

Invitation to godly living
Isaiah 55:1-9
Luke 14:1-14
John 3:1-16
John 15:1-17
Romans 12:1-8
Romans 12:9-21
2 Corinthians 9:6-15
Ephesians 6:10-20
Philippians 2:12-18
Colossians 3:1-11

God's good promises
Psalm 34:1-10
Psalm 62:5-8
Psalm 63:1-8
Luke 11:5-13
John 14:15-21

Joy of Christian living
Ephesians 3:14-20
Matthew 5:1-11
John 15:1-17
1 Corinthians 13
Philippians 1:3-11
Philippians 4:2-9
Colossians 1:9-14
2 Peter 1:3-11
1 John 4:7-21

Assurance in hardships
Psalm 23
Psalm 71:19-24
Psalm 77:1-15
Psalm 116
Psalm 124
Psalm 138
Romans 8:18-27
Romans 8:28-39
2 Corinthians 4:1-12

Praise
Psalm 33:1-11
Psalm 33:12-22
Psalm 47
Psalm 67
Psalm 93
Psalm 96
Psalm 97
Psalm 98
Psalm 99

Psalm 100
Psalm 103:1-8
Psalm 146
Psalm 147:1-11

Delight in God's will
Psalm 1
Psalm 19:7-14
Romans 8:12-17
Romans 12:9-21

Christian unity
John 17:20-26
1 Corinthians 1:10-17
1 Corinthians 3:1-15
1 Corinthians 12:12-31
Ephesians 4:1-13

Healing in sickness
2 Kings 5:1-15
John 4:46-54
John 5:1-19
James 5:13-20

Comfort in sorrow
Psalm 23
Isaiah 43:1-5
Isaiah 49:8-13
Isaiah 61:1-3
John 14:1-7
Romans 8:18-39
1 Corinthians 15:20-28
1 Corinthians 15:50-58
2 Corinthians 1:1-11
1 Thessalonians 4:13-18
2 Thessalonians 2:13-17
Hebrews 4:14-16
Revelation 7:9-17
Revelation 21:1-5

21. The Importance of Follow-up Care

The importance of follow-up care cannot be overemphasized. You are a blessing to your members not only by what you say in your visits but also by who you are: a shepherd of God's people. Your very office is an assurance to the members that they belong to the body of Christ.

Whenever something noteworthy is mentioned or discussed at one of your visits, follow up a few days later and ask about further developments. Follow-up care validates your initial pastoral outreach. Your people feel affirmed and respected when you make a second contact. They conclude that your first visit meant as much to you as it did to them. Follow-up contact can include making another brief visit or a phone call, or sending an e-mail or a note. The recipient will conclude, if only subconsciously, "Our elder is a person who cares."

Follow Up
You will invariably find that follow-up gestures are appreciated in much greater proportion to the investment of your time.

Sadly, the reverse may be true too: when your members don't hear from you much at all, they may wonder how deeply you care about their well-being.

22. Chance Encounters as Ministry Opportunities

Of course, we understand that nothing happens by chance. However, you will have ministry opportunities that are entirely unplanned. Don't underestimate the importance of these "chance encounters." You may be busy with something else, but ministry is often accomplished by such "interruptions."

Regularly checking your log or index system will keep you aware of your members and their circumstances. When you see them at congregational activities or spot one of them in the neighborhood shopping center, say hello. If you both have the time, take a few minutes to chat. Ask about the member's well-being. Add a word of encouragement. Make a mental note of important details and record them in your log later.

You may find that using such encounters constructively makes you a more outgoing and fulfilled person. And it means a lot to your people when they know you take the time to care. Ongoing contact is the very vehicle of your ministry.

Pay special attention to the children in your district. Know their names. Make them feel special by singling them out and paying attention to them. It is important for them to know that they too belong to the church.

Think of these chance encounters as divine appointments. Indeed, they occur according to God's divine will and should not lightly be ignored or avoided.

23. A Word About Boundaries

You approach the members of your district as an officebearer. The fact that you are an elder means that the office is a fence, or boundary, between you. Such a boundary doesn't separate you; it makes ministry possible. Robert Frost wrote, "Good fences make good neighbors." Similarly good boundaries make good ministry. Propriety and respect must always characterize your contacts. Don't be overly formal, but avoid excessive familiarity, which can lead to emotional dependence and even romantic involvement. Draw firm boundaries around your person and your actions as an elder.

Also draw a boundary line around the power and influence that you as an officebearer possess. Use whatever influence you may have for the promotion of the kingdom rather than for promoting your personal agenda or position.

The church has its own built-in boundaries without which it cannot function effectively. Church task forces, small groups, committees, and leaders have their assigned responsibilities. As the consistory and council consider various initiatives, they must ask, "Which board, committee, or person will handle these tasks?" Don't overstep the boundaries of others' responsibilities.

Things that members have told in confidence should never be revealed to third parties. It is a good practice not to talk about anything that you are privy to because of your office. You may go a step further: make it a personal rule that whatever you discuss with your members you keep to yourself. If people share information with you that you feel should be shared with others, seek permission first. See section 45 for further advice on discretion and confidentiality.

Consider also a boundary of a different sort. In your district ministry you will regularly be confronted with parishioners' problems. Place a boundary between you and those problems. Maintain the boundary between your personal life and your life as an officebearer. Don't be active in the one at the expense of the other. Seek a healthy balance. Your members are actually not helped when you assume responsibility for their needs, as they may assume an unhealthy dependence. Go easy on giving advice. Your ministry will be of more value when assuring members that they are whole in the sight of their heavenly Father and are of good standing among God's people.

Special Guidelines Regarding Sexual Boundaries

▶ Be vigilant about the dynamics of sexuality in your relationships with parishioners and colleagues. Your position may invite temptations. Those whom you serve have their own needs and expectations. Deal with them respectfully and circumspectly.

▶ Safeguard healthy relationships in practical ways. If you are visiting a member of the opposite sex, take along your spouse or a fellow elder. Visit early in the evening rather than late. Should these safeguards not be possible in a situation, try to visit in a church facility with other people around rather than in a deserted building. Meet in a room with uncovered windows and keep doors ajar.

▶ Agree to be accountable to a colleague, spouse, or peer to ensure that you are maintaining proper boundaries.

▶ Guard your spiritual, emotional, and physical well-being. Do your work with a positive, charitable attitude. Grudges and discontent will undercut your defense against temptation and self-destruction. Draw on the resources of faith and prayer to surmount discouragement, criticism, and loss of self-esteem—conditions that make you a ready target for the evil one.

24. Visiting Single Members

As many as half of the people in your district may be single, divorced, or widowed. Although the observations and suggestions in the previous part hold true for single members as well as traditional families, visiting single members involves other considerations as well.

Things to Keep in Mind

▶ A single person may be intimidated by having two visitors; a one-on-one visit is often more effective.

▶ Many consistories wisely prohibit visits between members of the opposite sex. If your consistory has both male and female elders and/or deacons, this can be easily dealt with. If there are no female officebearers, your council would be wise to appoint and train godly women to make visits to single women. If your church does allow visits between members of the opposite sex, you'll want to arrange such visits at a public place such as a restaurant, church office space (with open door), or some other suitable public area. An elder cannot be too cautious in this area, both to guard against any temptation and to prevent any misunderstanding.

▶ Personal pastoral care can be provided in a variety of settings. Some single members may not want to visit with you at all. They may prefer another form of personal interaction, such as a group meeting or prayer circle. In fact, the trend among members in general seems to be to seek pastoral affirmation in such settings rather than through the traditional home visit. As a district elder, make sure you attend group meetings occasionally in order to maintain contact with your members.

▶ Single people may deal with life situations and challenges that are unfamiliar to you. Be a careful listener and a quick and sympathetic learner. Are single members lonelier than married people? Some may be, but others may not be lonely at all. They may have a variety of satisfying friendships. Try to understand how this person is doing and affirm him or her in the promises of Jesus. Find out whether this person feels welcomed by the church community. Be aware that sometimes single members are made to feel like second-class members by thoughtless or unguarded remarks from those who are married. Remember that the church community is composed of families and singles; your church program and ministry practice should include both groups.

Single Parents

Of special concern to you will be the single parents in your district. Life under normal circumstances can be hard, but single parents face additional problems and burdens. They miss the counsel and consolation husbands and wives can provide. They often struggle with feelings of fear, fatigue, worry, regret, anger, and rejection. Their income may be limited. They face all the demands of raising children alone. Meaningful friendships may be hard to establish. Logistical problems are harder to solve, and the work is never done. Moments of rest and reflection are rare.

So it's a good idea to place single parents on top of the list for regular contact, as well as widows, widowers, and the poor. Enlist the pastoral and material help of the deacons as you minister to these people's unique circumstances.

Note: See also section 26, "Ministry to the Elderly" and section 34, "Ministry to the Bereaved."

25. Calling on People Who Are Ill

Illness may bring discomfort and pain, but it can also create secondary problems in such areas as personal faith, family, marriage, work, economic well-being, and so on.

Sickness and pain are frequently mingled with vague feelings of guilt and failure. Those who are sick often experience fear, and fear can immobilize people. Discussing their illness helps to relieve the fear and restores the sick to good confidence and courage—that's why James advised sick people to "call the elders of the church to pray" with them (James 5:13-16). The form for the Ordination of Elders and Deacons advises elders to "bear up God's people in their pain and weakness."

Things to Keep in Mind

▶ The word *health* is related to the word *whole*. People with illness experience a lack of wholeness not only in their body but also in their inner being. They may not feel whole as persons. That's why your ministry to the sick should first be one of *affirmation*: remind this person that he or she is whole in Christ and has a place in the community of believers.

▶ Your visits, prayers, and general support are crucial to the healing process. Remember that you represent Christ the healer. Let the person you're visiting know that you are visiting as an official representative of the church community by saying something like "I've come to visit you as your elder." This makes it clear that your visit is not just that of a friend, but as a representative of Christ and his church.

▶ Be informed. Don't pretend to be a medical authority, but take careful note of what the patient chooses to entrust to you. Be discreet when asking details. Let people be their own judge of what to tell you about their illness and medical procedures.

▶ Avoid giving the impression that you are in a hurry to leave, but don't overstay your welcome. Sick people generally prefer a short visit of fifteen minutes or so. If you sense that the person would like you to stay a bit longer, ask!

▶ When the illness is of longer duration, make regular visits. You may wish to keep contacts somewhat varied: intersperse visits with phone calls and cards or personal notes. If a person doesn't hear from you for an extended time, you cannot hope to be of great significance in his or her life.

▶ Remember that sickness can affect a believer's faith life. He or she may wonder about many things: What is the purpose of this trial? What role does prayer play in my healing? Do I deserve this sickness? Why does the pain continue? Are there spiritual reasons for my pain? How does God figure into my illness?

▶ Don't attempt to answer these hard questions, but do sympathize with these struggles of the soul. Do more listening than talking. Avoid pat answers, but don't hesitate to assure the sick person that God is near, that God is faithful, that God hears our prayers, and that God is endless in compassion and love.

From the Word

Here are some passages from the Psalms you may want to read to provide comfort:

Psalms 23:4; 27:1, 13-14; 62:1, 7-8; 71:1-3; 77:10-15; 91:1-6; 116:1-7; 118:28-29; 121:1-2, 7-8. See also the list of Bible passages in section 20.

▶ Avoid talking about yourself. If the patient inquires about you, answer politely but briefly.

▶ Chronically ill people may need your help to keep in touch with the life of the Christian community. Explore ways to keep communication lines open. Ask if the patient would like you to arrange for others to visit regularly.

▶ Keep your closing prayer brief. Center on the well-being of the sick person without spelling out medical details. Pray for healing when appropriate, for strength, courage, endurance, and the nearness of God. Invite the person to express a prayer request. When appropriate, it can be a healing gesture to hold the person's hand while praying. This touch conveys care and represents Christ's own healing touch.

Hospital Calls

You will also call on patients in hospitals, nursing homes, and hospice care. In these settings, with busy doctors and nurses hurrying about, you may feel out of place or in the way. Again, remember that you are representing Christ the healer, and that your spiritual care has an important place in the healing process. That's why many hospitals have chaplains.

- Begin by letting the person know that you are making this visit in your capacity as an elder, and therefore as an extension of the healing ministry of the church. For example, you may say something like: "Hello, I'm your elder. I wanted to visit you here to pray for you and to help you experience Christ's healing love and the care of the entire congregation."

- Keep the visit brief (see the fifteen-minute rule above). Talk with the person, then read an appropriate passage of Scripture and lead in prayer. As you leave, mention that you will be back soon.

- A patient may wish to explain hospital policies and medical procedures. Pay careful attention, but avoid expressing your opinions or being drawn too deeply into the discussion. Be discreet with the questions you ask.

- Acquaint yourself with the hospital's visiting regulations. Never sit on the person's hospital bed, as this is an invasion of the patient's space and may even cause pain. Find a chair.

- You may not be the only visitor. When a number of people are visiting, they may begin to talk among themselves, and the patient may no longer be focus of the visit. If this happens, don't hesitate to shorten your visit and tell the person you'll come back another time. You may want to ask the all the visitors if you can lead in prayer.

> Here are some questions to ask when you visit:
>
> - How can I pray for you?
>
> - How can the church help support your family at this time?
>
> - What kinds of doubts or fears have you been experiencing?
>
> - How have you met God through what has happened?

Health Care Precautions

When visiting patients in a health care facility, be sure to practice good hygiene. Wash your hands as you enter a patient's room, and again when you leave. This prevents spreading disease. If you are sick yourself, even with just a cold, you should not visit a sick person. Get your influenza shot annually to protect yourself and the people you visit. Patients have died from diseases like influenza that are brought in by visitors.

26. Ministry to the Elderly

They worked hard, they did much for the church, they developed many skills, but now they may feel superfluous, unneeded, and, at times, lonely. They are the elderly in your congregation. Their number is growing as the entire population ages. In some churches, seniors make up 20 to 40 percent of the congregation.

Things to Keep in Mind

▶ The elderly appreciate regular visits. They would like you to come often, and they wouldn't mind if you stayed a little longer. That's why, as a district elder, you need to be assisted by other members to make these visits. The council should make these arrangements. Some churches supplement the elder's care with that of a care team of trained, unordained members.

▶ Elderly members may struggle with faith problems just as younger members of the congregation do. They may feel insecure of their redemption. Some may feel attacked by powers of darkness. Your job is to "encourage the aged to persevere in God's promises," according to the elder's ordination form. Tactfully invite elderly members to share their spiritual concerns with you.

▶ Involve elderly members in church life. Look for ways they can serve. See to it that all printed church materials reach their mailboxes and homes. Be sure to seek the advice of the elderly on congregational issues. Remember that your elderly members have much experience and, in many cases, much wisdom. They have heard and pondered many sermons and may be well-equipped to provide care for each other. It may take an encouraging word from you to give them the freedom to minister in this way. Church leaders should be careful not to patronize the elderly but rather to respect and esteem them.

▶ The elderly face a sobering reality: many of their contemporaries have died. They experience a world that is constantly changing. But it is a myth that old people cannot or will not change. They desire to be worthy participants in the processes that cause change (see also "Report of the Committee on Senior Ministries," *Acts of Synod 1985*, p. 702).

Care Facilities

A growing number of the elderly members of your church will live in nursing homes or places of assisted living. They will appreciate your visits more than ever before. They may feel somewhat starved for news. In this case, don't hesitate to do what you avoid in "ordinary" visits: make some small talk. As always, when arranging your visits, make sure that you respect the facility's visiting guidelines. (See also section 25.)

Who Will Visit?

One congregation arranged visits for the elderly and shut-ins according to a four-month cycle that is regularly repeated:

- Month 1: a visit from the district elder

- Month 2: a visit from the pastor

- Month 3: a visit from a member of the congregational visiting team

- Month 4: a visit from a deacon

27. Ministry to Youth

The spiritual health of the children and teens in your church is of great importance. If the younger generation is not a vital part of your congregation, your church life will suffer. Care for the young should be both pastoral (focusing on personal guidance) and programmatic (focusing on structured group activities). The ordination form urges elders to "be a friend and Christlike example to children. Give clear and cheerful guidance to young people." (See Church Order, Art. 63 for a statement on the importance of ministry to youth.)

Spiritual Formation

The great challenge for the church is to assist in the spiritual formation of its youth by providing an effective personal ministry program, maintaining a solid teaching program, and promoting fellowship and friendships. Adopting challenging service programs will prove helpful too.

A youth leader recently remarked that a critical issue for young people is the interaction between the Christian family and secular society. The Christian family bases its values, language, and ideas on the Word of God. It expects allegiance and loyalty from its members. Society, on the other hand, offers competing values and alluring rewards. Young people must come to terms with this dilemma. Will they be defined by the family's expectations or by the world's enticement? Young people struggle to understand who they are. They wonder about issues of sexual awareness and experience. They search for a framework of values in which they can find peace and security.

What Can You Do?

Emphasize the importance of ministry to the young in consistory and council meetings. Encourage your pastor to take a deep personal interest in the children and young people of the church. Consider whether your commitment to children and teens is adequately reflected in your church's budget.

Church Order Article 63 stipulates that elders bear responsibility for the faith nurture of the children and youth of the congregation. That means elders should be aware of the curricula used for Sunday school and other education programs. Do these curricula reflect a Reformed understanding of the Bible and Reformed doctrines? It is also wise for elders to visit various church school classes (by prior arrangement with the teacher or leader) to see what is being taught and to show support of the education programs for children and youth.

▶ Show interest in the church's youth programs. Talk to youth leaders now and then. Drop in at youth-oriented events occasionally. Stop by the young people's meetings for a few moments and speak a word of encouragement. Don't leave these gestures only to the youth elder.

▶ Get to know the children and teens of your district. Know their names and keep records of events that are important to them. Maintain a comfortable level of contact with them. Be available for them. Once a trust relationship develops, they will feel free to talk about spiritual things with you. In later life they will remember you as a source of blessing. Can you think of a richer legacy?

▶ Pray for the children and youth of your congregation. Church Order Article 63 stipulates that prayer for children and youth is an obligation of every church.

▶ Incorporate children and youth fully in the worship and ministry of the church. Many of your young people are willing and capable workers. You will find that the church leaders do more than minister to young people; they minister with young people. Youth elders and/or a youth director should remain close to young people but they should not take over for them. The focus of the work of elders and staff should be on spiritual guidance, encouragement, and empowerment. (See also *Guiding the Faith Journey,* Faith Alive Christian Resources, pp. 105-107.)

Young Members Who Live at a Distance

You will find it very rewarding to pay special attention to your young members at local and distant colleges, in the military, or in other institutions. Try to keep in contact with them as much as you can, with the help of the church's ministry team. Arrange for volunteers to correspond with them regularly. Make sure these young members get the same printed materials the other church members get.

A Youth Elder's Extra Step

Youth elder Bart ministered thoughtfully to the parents of a young member who was giving them grief. Gradually he discovered that they were not alone in their struggles—several other parents lay awake at night worrying over their kids. He alerted their district elders to visit them.

Two things became clear: the problems in which these young people found themselves were complex and varied; and the parents, some of whom were consistory members, suffered mostly in silence.

Care for Members Who Have Moved

The council of one congregation appointed a small task force to conduct a survey of their young members who had left the area to settle elsewhere. The study group checked membership transfer records, compared notes with the parents as appropriate, and contacted the young members whenever possible. The outcome was disappointing: one-third of the young members who had moved no longer attended church.

The council then appointed a small task force to maintain contact with all young members in the military, at distant colleges and universities, and in other places. The task force recruited volunteers to write them and keep them informed about congregational life. The pastor began a monthly e-mail newsletter especially for college and university students, keeping them up to date on church life and addressing the issues they were facing on campus. Most students expressed strong appreciation for these efforts.

28. Ministry with People with Disabilities

About 18 percent of the people in Canada and the United States live with disability. The word *disability* includes various impairments:

▶ mobility, usually resulting in the need to use a cane, walker, or wheelchair

▶ cognitive, such as Down syndrome or autism

▶ emotional, such as bipolar disorder or schizophrenia

▶ sensory, including primary visual or hearing impairments

▶ diminishing abilities associated with aging

▶ chronic illnesses, including chronic pain

A Great Challenge

Without realizing it, churches erect various barriers to the full and effective participation of people with disabilities in the life of the church. These barriers include architectural, attitudinal, and communications barriers. For example, many churches are built with steps rather than ramps and without an accessible bathroom. Many churches structure their youth programming for typical children and youth, to the exclusion of children with autism and Down syndrome. Many churches ask people to rise for singing to lyrics projected on an overhead screen, excluding people who cannot stand. Usually unintentionally, people with disabilities are left out of the life and ministry of the congregations. Churches should continually ask themselves if their "shut-ins" are not in reality "shut-outs."

Scripture teaches that all people are made in the image of God, and that all believers are part of the body of Christ. The New Testament says pointedly, "Those parts of the body that seem to be weaker are indispensable" (1 Cor. 12:22). Therefore, ministry with people with disabilities begins with a warm welcome and progresses to encouragement to discern and employ their gifts in ministry. This perspective moves away from a needs-based model of disability to a strengths-based model, from a deficit model to a partner model. That's why this section is titled "Ministry *with* People with Disabilities," not "Ministry *to* People with Disabilities."

A Challenge

Living with a disability or with a loved one who has a disability can present special challenges including isolation, loss of self-esteem, stress on a marriage, financial pressures, and troubled faith in God's goodness. Caring council members will seek to discern those needs and mobilize members to help meet those needs.

Including people with disabilities in the life and ministry of the church involves a cost of time, energy, and resources. But the benefits are many, including worship that gives glory to God in new ways, enhanced fellowship, more hospitable outreach, and, most important, obedience to the commands of Scripture.

How You Can Help

▶ Visit the people in your church who have disabilities, not only to learn their needs but also to discern their gifts and to help them discover ways to be of service to God.

▶ Conduct an audit of the accessibility of your buildings, programs, and communications. Be sure to consider transportation needs of people with disabilities and older people of the congregation.

▶ With the council, you may wish to study *A Compassionate Journey: Coming Alongside People with Disabilities or Chronic Illnesses* by John Cook and *90% of Helping Is Just Showing Up* by James Kok.

▶ Consider setting up a Friendship group in your church. This can be done in partnership with neighboring congregations. Friendship's mission is "to share God's love with people who have cognitive impairments and to enable them to become an active part of God's family."

▶ Encourage young people and adults with disabilities to make profession of faith.

▶ Look for specific ways that people with disabilities can serve in the church.

▶ Adopt the "Church Policy on Disabilities" available from the CRC Office of Disability Concerns.

29. Ministry to Those Who Suffer Abuse

Tragically, children and adults are abused in the home, in the community, and worst of all, in the church and by other Christians. These incidents of abuse represent some of the most difficult pastoral situations.

Abuse occurs in various forms:

▶ Physical abuse is any non-accidental injury inflicted on another person. It is often a chronic pattern of behavior. In some cases, severe punishment is a form of abuse.

▶ Sexual abuse is the exploitation of a person, regardless of age or circumstance, for the sexual gratification of another. Sexual gratification, however, is often less important than the feeling of power that sexual abuse gives to the abuser. Sexual abuse includes physical and nonphysical contact. For example, fondling a person's breasts or genitals is physical contact, while photographing a nude child in graphic poses is nonphysical contact.

▶ Emotional abuse is using threats or silence to manipulate or control another. Emotional abuse diminishes another's self-esteem and demands dependency on the abuser. Emotional abuse is chronic and may continue for a longer time than other abuses.

The impact of all forms of abuse is devastating. For a victim of abuse, the spiritual and emotional damage lasts long after the abuse ends.

In abuse situations, the abuser has power over the victim. This power comes from superior size or strength or from a position of authority like a parent to child or teacher to student. Power can also have a

The Prevalence of Abuse

The problem of abuse is greater than most people think. The Calvin College Social Research Center conducted a survey of abuse in 1990. The survey reported that 12% of adults in the Christian Reformed Church were victims of physical abuse or neglect; 13% of CRC adults were victims of sexual abuse; and 19% were victims of emotional abuse. Stunningly, 15% of CRC adults claimed they had committed at least one form of abuse. The research also showed that some offenders were victims in childhood.

spiritual source, such as an officebearer who uses Scripture to control or exploit a parishioner. When people misuse legitimate forms of power and authority, the result is a betrayal of trust. Such betrayal by Christians leaves deep spiritual wounds in the victim. A victim of abuse may need years to rebuild this lost trust, and some never do. When the offender is a church leader, many victims seek healing away from the congregation or denomination. Sadly, but understandably, some victims leave the church altogether. In this case, Jesus' words about the millstone (Matthew 18:6) are frighteningly appropriate.

The Elder's Role with a Victim of Abuse

▶ Believe the victim's story until facts prove otherwise. Abuse thrives in secrecy. Rarely are there witnesses to abuse. In addition, the victim is often threatened, bribed, or coerced into keeping the secret—sometimes for many years after the incident occurred. When a victim discloses a story of abuse to an elder, believing the story may be the first step in restoring the trust betrayed by the offender.

▶ Do not investigate the story yourself. The elder's role is to provide support, comfort, advocacy, and to seek justice and reconciliation when possible. Elders who investigate abuse matters may find themselves at odds with the victim, the offender, or the church. An investigation into the allegations is crucial, but it should be conducted by a competent investigator from the community.

▶ Elders can be a resource for victims of abuse. They should be familiar with books, videos, or articles on abuse; they should be knowledgeable about counselors or therapists to whom they can refer victims of abuse. Elders can consult with denominational personnel in the Abuse Prevention office for advice. In addition, some classes have appointed a Safe Church Team with local representatives.

▶ Elders should model appropriate boundaries with victims. This is important so that the victim feels safe during meetings and conversations. Be respectful of intimacy issues and refrain from hugs or touches that might confuse the victim as to your intentions. Elders should pace the conversation so that information is disclosed when it is comfortable, not upon demand or "in the interest of time." Further, elders should allow the expression of anger and sadness—repeatedly. Abuse leaves scars that can heal over time. But during that time, the victim may need to express the anguish over and over again. There are few shortcuts around the pain of abuse.

- Elders should learn about ecclesiastical processes. The Manual of Church Government, updated in 2008, gives direction for responding to allegations and confessions of misconduct or ungodly conduct (see Art. 78-84). Elders, along with deacons, have authority to adjudicate such complaints. It is a moral obligation to know what processes exist; it is also a duty to know and understand the processes when called upon to exercise them.

- Sadly, in some cases, the abuse has been perpetrated by a fellow church officebearer: pastor, elder, or staff person. In such cases, it is extremely important that elders strictly follow the guidelines of the Church Order, seek the help of the classis, and seek the help of the denominational offices of Abuse Prevention and Pastor-Church Relations.

What Synod Said

Synod approved two sets of guidelines to follow when a person alleges abuse by a church leader. One set of guidelines lays out the steps to follow when a child alleges abuse. These guidelines emphasize the importance of complying with local laws and working with police officials and child protection agencies. Elders should be familiar with the child protection laws in their community.

The other guidelines lay out the steps to follow when an adult alleges abuse. These guidelines involve the Classis Safe Church Team, which conducts an advisory panel into the allegations. The panel reports their findings to the council. In the council room, elders need to set aside their personal opinions about the alleged victim and the alleged offender, and instead respond to the report as presented by a trained advisory panel.

Pastoral Considerations

Abuse matters are highly emotional and tend to be complicated and chaotic. For these reasons, they become very difficult for elders. Victims and their families express feelings of anger, confusion, fear, distrust, and shame. The victim often feels isolated and, unfortunately, has often been the target of derision by others in the congregation or community. Elders must also be sensitive to the polarizing effect that abuse incidents have on the congregation. The strong feelings and chaos affect relationships among council members too. These are reasons to seek advice from denominational personnel trained in this area.

However, elders should not shy away from these difficult situations. They will handle them better if they increase their awareness of the dynamics of abuse. Book knowledge does not compare with attendance at training sessions. If church leaders do not take the opportunity to learn, inevitably they will get the opportunity to face the issue again with no less heartache than the first time.

Another pastoral consideration is to work for the implementation of a child safety policy to reduce the risk of abuse occurring. The policy sets out the procedures for screening volunteers and reporting allegations of abuse. Those procedures can effectively reduce the church's liability if an allegation arises. A set of policies and procedures for responding to allegations by an adult victim would also serve the church well. For information about developing and implementing a child safety policy, see *Preventing Child Abuse: Creating Safe Places* by Beth A. Swagman (Faith Alive Christian Resources). For more information and resources contact the CRC Office of Abuse Prevention (see Appendix).

30. Ministry to Homosexual Members

Homosexuality is more prevalent among Christian Reformed church members than was generally assumed. Various synods have stated that our churches, by and large, have failed to respond adequately to the needs of their gay and lesbian members. The anxiety and emotional suffering of such members will probably never be fully appreciated by those unacquainted with these realities. Traditionally, homosexuals suffered disapproval, rejection, and even ridicule. In many cases that led to feelings of guilt, shame, and fear. Added to their burden were the stereotypes and falsehoods that arose about them over time.

Some homosexuals have testified that through prayer and therapy they became heterosexual. Many more, however, declared that their condition was no more removed by prayer than Paul's thorn in the flesh (2 Cor. 12:7). Pastoral caregivers should realize that same-sex orientation does not constitute a gay person's total identity, much as a heterosexual person is not completely defined by his or her sexual orientation. The church must seek to empower members to own their sexual identity and yet live beyond it.

Can homosexual members serve as officebearers? Yes, synod said. "Churches should recognize that their homosexual members are fellow-servants of Christ who are to be given opportunity to render within the office and structures of the congregation the same service that is expected from heterosexuals" (*Acts of Synod 1973*, p. 52).

Ministry to homosexual members requires not only pastoral sensitivity but also a high degree of understanding what homosexuality is about. You may find considerable help in two studies conducted by the

A Distinction

Synod 1973 made a distinction between *homosexuality* and *homosexualism*. Homosexuality, it said, denotes the condition in which one is sexually oriented toward persons of the same sex. The homosexual member might bear little or no responsibility for this condition. Homosexuality may be the result of abnormalities in the parent-child relationship (the *nurture* component), or it may stem from genetic-biological factors (the *nature* component). Homosexualism denotes the explicit practice of this sexual orientation. Synod found homosexualism to be incompatible with the will of God.

Christian Reformed synods of 1973 and 1999. These studies can be found on pages 609-633 of the *Acts of Synod 1973* and pages 237-279 of the *Acts of Synod 1999*.

Pastoral Guidelines for Elders

▶ Provide care that will foster a sense of equality of all members—married, single, young, and old. Small group ministry teams and prayer groups can offer a place of belonging and equality where homosexual members can find safety and be encouraged to be of good hope in Christ. All members, heterosexual as well as homosexual, will find strength there to face sexual temptation.

▶ Pastoral caregivers should do their utmost to make homosexual members feel wholeheartedly accepted by the church community as persons for whom Christ died and rose. Ministry to these members must be marked by priestly compassion and concern. They must be assured that their participation in the church's program is as eagerly sought as that of other members. All members must be given the opportunity to serve the Master in various capacities and with equal honor.

▶ Caregivers should feel a special concern for parents of homosexual members. The parents often bear the burden of prejudicial attitudes on the part of other church members. Elders should do whatever they can to dispel prejudice and foster a loving and supportive environment.

31. Ministry to Those Struggling with Addiction

There will be some members in your congregation who struggle with addiction. Can you help them break the addiction cycle? Probably not. Addictions and their resultant afflictions are incredibly complex and need professional intervention. But you can be a friend and companion to these brothers and sisters as they battle addiction.

Addictions come in a bewildering array of forms: pornography, betting and gambling, eating disorders, sexual addiction, and more—each with its own bitter price to pay.

Equally ruinous, if not worse, are dependence on various forms of prescription and nonprescription drugs, including narcotics (such as cocaine, codeine, or morphine), hallucinogens (such as barbiturates or amphetamines), alcohol, and nicotine.

Ingesting any of these leads to dependence because of changes in brain functioning. It is as if the brain assumes a personality of its own, eagerly lusting for whatever substance it has focused on. The sought-for *high* is usually followed by a *crash*, which produces its own stronger craving for another *fix*. The addicted person is dragged along in this desperate cycle of near-helplessness.

Secondary results of addiction include emotional and physical suffering, broken relationships, financial ruin, loss of job and business, and, of course, the paralysis of guilt.

How Can Elders Help?

▶ Remember that time is of the essence. Treatment delayed is treatment weakened. If there ever was a time that an individual elder needs to seek the help and advice of the pastor

The Cycle

Those recently caught in the web of addiction will almost invariably experience denial. Next, they will be convinced that they can handle the problem on their own, and they will have every intention to break free. Family members are often instrumental in breaking the cycle of denial. Encourage the addict to have a medical checkup. Perhaps the advice of a trusted physician will motivate him or her to seek treatment.

and fellow elders, it is now. If your congregation includes people who have counseling skills, check with them, seek their advice, and, where appropriate, seek their help.

▶ Addicts are lonely people, so seek them out regularly. Even the most frustrating visit is better than no visit at all. Those of us who by God's grace have escaped addiction cannot begin to imagine the depth of the forsakenness they feel. Remember that you are not an expert on addiction. Be careful not to dispense advice. Be patient. Assure the person of your loyalty, your friendship, and your love. Do whatever you can to draw addicts into the fellowship of believers. Their family members struggle with their own problems, questions, and distress. Seek them out too. Let them tell you their story. You cannot heal their addiction, but your willingness to listen is a great help.

▶ Be aware that addicts tend to be manipulative. Their entire inner mental life is focused on satisfying the deep craving for the next fix. All the faculties of mind and soul are geared to satisfying the addiction. Conscience becomes nearly nonfunctional. To an addict, references to sin are not helpful. Addicts have condemned themselves for sin and guilt over and over. Assure them of God's grace and God's offer of forgiveness in Christ.

While Alcoholics Anonymous and its many Twelve Step children are not explicitly Christian in their approach (they call God the "Higher Power"), a close examination of the material shows that it's based on the Christian doctrines of grace, repentance, fellowship, and restitution. Consider opening your church to a community Twelve Step group. There is also an excellent explicitly Christian Twelve Step small group guide available online: *The Twelve Steps: A Spiritual Journey.*

▶ There are many people and institutions in the healing profession who can provide effective treatment, as well as Twelve Step programs dealing with the many particular forms of addiction, from substances to sex. Information regarding the nature and treatment of addiction can be found (in varying qualities) on the Internet.

▶ It has been demonstrated over and over that treatment programs must not be ended prematurely against the advice of expert caregivers. Even those who have enjoyed healing (and there are many who are thus blessed) will continue to sense an underlying craving. By God's grace and the support of the Christian community, they need not yield.

32. Ministry to Those with Marriage Problems

Can you minister effectively to couples struggling with marriage problems? Yes, you can. Remember, however, that you are not a marriage counselor. You may be equipped to discuss common marriage problems, and you may even give helpful advice, but when it becomes clear that a couple faces a serious rift, suggest that they seek the help of a competent marriage therapist.

There are many excellent Christian therapists, and they should certainly be utilized where available. However, being a Christian does not guarantee competence in therapy. Many communities do not have competent, well-trained Christian therapists, and that should never keep people in need from seeking therapy. Competent and well-trained therapists should honor the religious and moral values of their clients no matter what their personal convictions.

Does referral to a counselor end your ministry to the couple? No. You should continue to minister to the couple in the name of Christ. Show that you are there for them by visiting and inquiring about their well-being. They may or may not want to share details of their therapy with you, but perhaps you can give them spiritual guidance and encouragement.

What the Elder Can Do

▶ Stay close to the couple with marriage problems. They tend to avoid contact with others and will often experience a sense of isolation and loneliness. Your expression of concern will address a deeply felt need. Early in your ministry to this couple, you may wish to ask them whether they would like the minister to be informed about your mutual visiting arrangement. Should the couple wish the minister to be part of the pastoral consultation, great. But that need not necessarily be so.

▶ Assure the couple that God loves them. When husband and wife feel isolated from each other, they may well feel isolated from God. God's love is unconditional. The couple may not have foreseen the trouble that has entered their marriage. Now they feel unworthy, betrayed, bewildered, and afraid.

▸ Remain impartial. Don't assign blame to either partner. Direct the partners to examine their own ways critically and, where appropriate, to confess wrongs to each other and to God. Weaknesses and shortcomings, once considered and confessed, are forgiven and should not be held against the other.

▸ Explore with the couple whether they will agree to establishing the following arrangement. With your help, both husband and wife select a mentor or a spiritual advisor: a man for the husband, a woman for the wife. The two mentors should be selected for their spiritual maturity and personal wisdom. They should be secure people who are sympathetic and compassionate, but also firm and candid. Husband and wife agree to establish honest relationships with their mentors and to consult with them in every significant step taken or decision made. From time to time you may arrange for a group meeting of the couple, the mentors, and yourself.

▸ There may come a point, especially when progress is slow or cooperation minimal, that you have to ask one or both partners whether they are having an affair. Don't hesitate to confront this issue. If either husband or wife admits that this is indeed so, you face a situation for which the previous points are inadequate. The pastor should now be brought in if that has not been done previously. Healing is out of reach unless the affair is ended, sin is confessed earnestly, and professional help is sought seriously. Church discipline may be necessary if there is no repentance.

▸ Should the couple wish to work hard at restoration with the help of marriage therapists, continue pastoral care. If divorce becomes a reality, give as much care as the individual parties will welcome.

▸ The dynamics of marriage problems are complex. If you try to follow the steps outlined above and you find that you are not equal to the challenge, encourage the couple to seek professional help. Your role would then be that of a friend and companion along a rocky road.

▶ You will very likely have one or more divorced members in your district. The lives of divorced people are usually very difficult. In fact it has been said that their lives are harder than that of widowed people, who get more empathy from the community. Divorced people not only experience grief but usually must also deal with feelings of guilt and regret. You should not try to be their therapist, nor even their advisor, but, rather, affirm them in their belonging to the community and assure them of the Savior's love and acceptance. Regular visits will generally be deeply appreciated!

33. Ministry to Those with Economic Problems

Economic life has become more unpredictable than ever. In some sectors, fabulous profits accumulate; in others, good and able people are suddenly excluded from the economic cycle and left to subsist on greatly reduced incomes. Some of these unfortunate people may sit next to you in church on Sunday, and their number may well increase in the coming years.

These people struggle with loss, fear, depression, and the pain of rejection. There is no single way to minister to them. The officebearers must become aware of such people and devise forms of ministry in keeping with their needs. Above all, don't hesitate to take the initiative in visiting those in your district who are unemployed. Ask them how they are doing. Pray with them. In almost all cases, elders are not able to contribute significantly to solutions. Those who struggle with the pain of economic misfortune will not expect that from you.

Still, do explore some possibilities. Are there people in your congregation who specialize in financial management? If so, suggest that your members consult with them. You must also seek advice and possible assistance from the deacons. In more general terms, bring these economic challenges to the attention of the entire council. Perhaps there are members in the congregation who know of job possibilities. Remember, if one of your district members suffers financial hardship, the entire congregation hurts.

Continue also to minister to these members pastorally. They need to see you regularly. Encourage them, read Scripture with them, pray with them. Do whatever you can to keep them from becoming isolated from the congregation. You may also seek their permission to share their burdens with the other members of your district when appropriate.

34. Ministry to the Bereaved

Ministering to the bereaved is a difficult but often highly rewarding task. After many years in ministry I still feel uncertain of myself in consoling the grieving. However, you can be a blessing to sorrowing people without being a trained grief counselor.

The following thoughts may be of help to you:

▶ The bereaved may initially go through a stage of numbness. They cannot immediately absorb the reality of their loss. That's why recently bereaved persons may appear to be strong and well-composed. It is not helpful to praise the grieving person for his or her apparent strength and courage. Once the numbness wears off, the grief may overwhelm. Be alert to the stages of grief that may occur. Before acceptance becomes a reality, the bereaved may experience feelings of denial, helplessness, anger, and despair.

▶ Don't be solution-oriented in your ministry to those who mourn. You bring a measure of support, but you cannot alleviate grief. Even well-intended attempts in that direction may not be helpful. The place made empty because of the death of a spouse or child or friend cannot be filled. Grieving is not to be equated with sickness from which people need to be healed. Life changes after bereavement; it is unalterably different. For fellow church members to expect the bereaved to "get over" their grief is not helpful. Remember also that people grieve in different ways. Be sensitive to each person's unique way of experiencing the pain of loss.

▶ Literature on grieving points out that there are less-than-commendable ways of grieving. As with all human emotions and experiences, that is probably true. However, if you think it your duty to correct the grieving, you will probably make matters worse. Many grieving people come to a place of peace via painful detours. Many make "progress," then suffer setbacks. In the end they will be grateful that you were there for them. Avoid giving advice. Quietly tell of God's help in trouble and need. Refrain of telling of other instances of bereavement you have known, even your own.

▶ Bereaved people need strength to cope with and to adjust to irretrievable loss. Can you help? Yes, to a modest degree you can. Be sure to make yourself available. Be present to listen and to offer fellowship. It is helpful for a sorrowing person to tell his or her story. By sharing the details of how it happened and how it hurts, the bereaved person gains strength, a little bit at a time. The process will take some time. Let it happen.

▶ Be patient. Sorrow is a worthy component of your congregation's spiritual and emotional mix. You need not, even at a subconscious level, be eager to have it removed from the congregational scene. A congregation living with the reality of grief in its ranks will more readily depend on the Lord. So continue your loving companionship with grieving members without being worried about "progress." Those now grieving will be thankful for your assuring presence.

▶ When ministering to the bereaved, keep an eye on the calendar. Note the date of the loved one's death and his or her birthday. On those days the pain of grief hits hard. Let the bereaved know that you remember them. Certain times of year, such as Christmas and Thanksgiving, also accentuate the stark absence of the deceased. Note also that the second anniversary of the loss can be particularly hard for the survivors. They now realize fully that the irreversibility of death must be accepted. This is also the time when people assume that the bereaved are "over" their grief and should have returned to a "normal life." Stop by for a bit of reminiscing—it will be appreciated.

Additional Helps

A Practical Handbook for Ministry by Wayne E. Oates (1992, Westminster/John Knox Press, 1992), pp.137-140.

Waiting for Morning: Seeking God in Our Suffering by James R. Kok (1997, Faith Alive Christian Resources)

A Grace Disguised by Gerald Sittser (1998, Zondervan)

▶ In case of the death of a child you will realize that you can only distantly sense the depth of the parents' sorrow. Be modest in your expressions of sympathy. Remember also that the siblings have their own way of grieving. Sometimes even the parents are not fully aware of that reality. See if you can arrange a visit with the siblings separately and ask them how they are doing.

35. Ministry to the Dying

You may not be invited to sit at many deathbeds. Still, as an elder you must give prayerful attention to ministering to the dying and to the surviving loved ones. Here are a few important guidelines for your consideration:

▶ Those who are terminally ill have the right to accurate medical information, including the physicians' diagnosis and prognosis. If medical evidence suggests that a patient will die, he or she should be informed, though you are not the person to do that. You may, however, with due discretion, advise the family members accordingly. They and the doctors should decide how to proceed.

▶ Always be ready to listen carefully to what the dying person wants to tell you. When he or she expresses guilt or regret, don't respond with easy assurances. Such feelings are probably long-standing and weigh heavily on the patient. Give ample time for the person to confess whatever sins burden their hearts. Then, on behalf of Christ, your Sender, you may speak words of forgiveness, free and complete, through the blood of Christ. God will not remember these sins any longer. The slate is clean, as far as God is concerned. If possible, invite the patient to accept that forgiveness, then pray for assurance and express thanks to God for so great a salvation.

▶ Terminally ill people may express deep worry about the well-being of their loved ones. Such concerns should not be taken lightly. If possible, allow for some discussion and explanation.

▶ Minister also to the family members. Each will cope with the death of their loved one in a unique way. If possible, have them tell you how they feel and where they stand with the Lord. Loved ones and immediate relatives of the deceased will deeply appreciate your follow-up visits and other remembrances.

> **Helpful Passages**
>
> The following Scripture passages testify to God's care for his people:
>
> Psalm 23
> Psalm 37:25
> Psalm 121
> John 14:1-4
> John 17:13-18
> Romans 8:18-30
>
> Assure the dying of the reality of the unsurpassed bliss of eternal life with such passages as:
>
> 1 Corinthians 15:20-28, 50-58
> Revelation 7:9-17
> Revelation 21:1-4

36. Ministry to the Suicidal

It has become increasingly clear that the decision to attempt suicide is the outcome of unimaginable mental pain and has nothing to do with the sincerity of the victim's faith. Consider the following observations:

▶ People suffering from deep depression that results in suicidal tendencies will often send signals of distress. Their life's patterns may show sudden or gradual changes. They may quietly express that they are weary of dealing with depression. They may neglect taking medicines. They may take the initiative of having a will drawn up. They may say such things as "I'm tired of trying." They may want to stay in bed. Appetite will probably diminish. They may avoid human contacts.

▶ If family members alert you to such realities, advise them to seek competent professional help immediately. You may wish to consult with the pastor. People near someone contemplating suicide should not hesitate to ask, "Have you thought of taking your life?" When family members (or you) find that such a person avoids overtures of help, take the initiative to arrange professional intervention.

▶ As an elder, don't postpone acting on whatever signals come your way. Suicide is on the increase, especially among the young. Seek every opportunity to assure desperate people that God is a God of love, mercy, acceptance, forgiveness, help, solutions, and new possibilities. Maintain regular contact with them.

▶ Once you have established pastoral contact with the depressed person or his/her family members, a pressing question is, "Should you inform the appropriate health authorities of possible suicide risks?" This is a very difficult

Loving, Searching Questions

When you visit with someone who may be suicidal, ask questions like these: What do you think of the future? Do you have hope for life? Do you have plans for next summer? Are you enjoying your hobbies? Are you concerned about the company you work for, your family, your church? Have you experienced God's grace in Christ? Consistently evasive answers or lack of interest in anything relating to the future may indicate deep problems.

decision indeed. You may advise the parties involved to consult the family physician, the pastor, and experts in the mental health field.

▶ Ministry to the friends and family that are left behind when someone takes his or her life is very important and very difficult. Elders, ministers, and other qualified visitors should cooperate in these tasks. Second-guessing the eternal future of a victim of suicide is inappropriate. While the act of suicide is certainly sinful, those who commit suicide often do so under the strain of emotional and situational forces beyond their control. Firm assurances must be given that the act of suicide is as much covered by the Savior's blood and grace as any other human act for which we have no explanation.

37. Caring for Those Who Leave Your Church

Trickling Away

The number of people who trickle away from CRC churches is probably larger than we think. In 2008, the Christian Reformed *Yearbook* reported that

- those who left for other churches totaled 3,812;

- those who came to us from other churches totaled 3,893;

- those who came to us through evangelism totaled 3,293;

- those who were removed from the membership roles (so-called "reversions") totaled 673.

Taking births and deaths into consideration, the CRC could report a net "gain" of 4,400 members. That is a reason for thankfulness. That number, however, includes 3,672 newly baptized children. So growth of adult members is modest.

There probably are some people in your district whom you hardly ever see in church. Many churches have members who never attend worship or who attend sporadically. Youth leaders tell us that, especially among young people, many who move away from their local churches do not take up church membership elsewhere. Elders often don't know how to handle these issues, and many postpone taking any kind of action.

Why People Leave

Sometimes people leave your church because they've moved to a distant city. When this happens, send a friendly letter or make a phone call. Inquire about their well-being. Tactfully ask whether they're exploring the possibility of joining another church. Offer to help in any way you can, and wish them well.

Other times, though, people leave churches because of discontent. They stop attending and then just disappear from the congregation's radar screen. In a research paper titled "Church Drop-outs," Ian Findlay McIntosh of Austin Seminary observes that those who leave usually do so for one of four reasons:

▶ **Internal reasons.** These are often thoughtful people. They have struggled with faith problems. They may doubt God's existence, or think that, even if God did exist, he cannot be known. They may also maintain that a loving God would not require the suffering and death of his Son to atone for sin. Some have pointed to the widespread suffering in the world and ask, "How can God permit that?"

- ▶ **External reasons.** For these people, church life has lost its importance. They are drawn to "worldly" living, pleasure seeking, and materialism. And they probably began to move in a circle of "unchurched" friends. The change may have started when attendance at worship slackened and Sunday became a day of seeking enjoyment away from the church community.

- ▶ **Institutional reasons.** These members are at odds with the way church life is conducted. They may disagree with the church's administration, its ministry, or how funds are spent. More recently, worship style has become a point of tension. Some feel strongly about a traditional form of worship; others prefer a less formal style with a looser structure and more contemporary forms of music.

- ▶ **Interpersonal reasons.** These members simply don't feel at home in their congregation, mostly because they don't get along with some of their fellow members. The reasons may vary from personal dislike to real conflict. After some real or perceived offenses they see little point in staying. Some quietly leave. But sometimes other members are drawn into such conflict situations. Parties may be formed. Battle lines may be drawn. No church community is exempt from the possibility of anger and conflict.

In your ministry to these members it is good to find out which of the above categories would apply most closely to each individually. That would help you to determine your approach.

Unless people tell you why they left, it's not always easy to clearly identify their reasons. You may make discreet inquiries. In case of young people, can parents help? Does the previous district elder know? Does the church office have some information? Make a list of those who no longer attend. Some may continue living in the area, some may have moved elsewhere.

What Can the District Elder Do?

- ▶ Get the facts and make sure they are accurate. Then try to plan a visit. Be friendly, non-threatening, patient, gracious, and tactful. You may have to overcome some resistance to your proposal for a visit. Perhaps arranging breakfast or lunch in a restaurant may be more acceptable. If you feel the need to state a reason for your initial contact, just say that you would like to say hello on behalf of the church of which you are an elder.

- ▶ Remember that your primary aim is to build a relationship. This is the first of what will, you hope, be several short visits. This is time-consuming ministry, but very worth your while. Invite your guest to tell about him or herself. Show interest in the details of his or her life. Be alert when people express needs or tell you of hardships, problems, disappointments, and worries. As you leave, suggest that you would like to visit again some time. Keep a record of the main details of the visit.

▶ At this stage you need not talk about the Lord or about church membership unless the person brings the discussion around to matters of faith. Focus on finding out how the person is doing. Once you establish a congenial relationship, you may broach the reality of this person's relationship with the church or with the Lord. Ask whether he or she would mind talking about it.

The approach you use depends on which of the four categories, listed above, this person would fit most closely:

▶ When you minister to those whose membership has weakened because of *internal reasons* of faith, gently emphasize that many believers have known those problems. Remember also that you don't have all the answers and that you yourself sometimes struggle with doubts. Unless you have given it a great deal of study, you are probably not prepared to prove God's existence or rationally defend the faith. You should, however, freely offer a testimony of your own reasons for faith and its blessings in your life. If you discover that the person's faith struggles are beyond your ability to handle, you may try to arrange for a visit with the pastor or another member of the church who is able to deal with such struggles.

▶ When you minister to those whose membership has weakened because of *external reasons*, again offer testimony to the blessings and joy of faith in your own life and that of others. You may also suggest that life without God has no lasting foundation. Such a life will readily become one of self-service, and its rewards and pleasures will soon evaporate. Relationships in such a world are conditioned by what you can offer in return. Lead the discussion into the direction of the joy of having a good relationship with the Lord, who is the only Sustainer of life. Serving God brings satisfaction and fulfillment that will triumph over the trials and setbacks of life.

▶ When you minister to those whose memberships have weakened because of *institutional reasons*, try to find out which part of the church's ministry or program these members found unacceptable. Offer your services to explore their misgivings a bit further. Misunderstanding may well be a factor. Perhaps you can place their criticism in a more realistic perspective. You may consult with your fellow elders or pastor(s) whether the church would be prepared to meet the criticism. You should also ask whether these members have attended another church or found another church home. If so, and if it is a Christian church, then you need not try to change their minds.

▶ When you minister to those whose memberships have weakened because of *interpersonal reasons*, invite them to explain what it is that bothers them in their fellow members. Are they just feeling discontent and annoyance, or has there been an actual conflict? Do their complaints point to something seriously wrong in the church? Can they be motivated to resolve the strained relationship? Even the finest people have their shortcomings; that's why churches are always imperfect. In case of broader conflict situations, more officebearers need to be recruited to help find a solution. Mediation sessions may lead to a resolution. If every effort at reconciliation has been made and no resolution is found, ask if they've considered seeking membership in another Christian church.

What Next?

When people tell you that they simply do not wish to belong to your church anymore, you must decide as elders whether you will treat such a statement as

Thoughtful, Impartial Listening

When discussing issues of disagreement, it is very important that the elder not take sides in the matter. For example, saying "Right, I know just how you feel," or "I know a number of others who share your concern" will only fan the flames of discontent. Just listen and gently offer emotional support. If the issue or issues have been thoroughly discussed and decided upon, you should, without arguing, offer some reasons for the decision. If the matter has not been seriously discussed by the consistory, you should bring it there for consideration, promising to get back to the person making the complaint, again without taking sides.

a resignation. Rather than let the matter linger indefinitely, you may wish to consider the membership ended and inform the party accordingly. Be sure to wish them well. If you think it's appropriate, call them occasionally to inquire about their well-being, demonstrating your love as a Christian brother or sister. Remember also that the rest of the church body will appreciate knowing that your pastoral efforts have led to some completion and conclusion. A simple statement in the bulletin that a person has withdrawn from membership or has affiliated with another church will accomplish this notification.

Council and Consistory

In Part 3 we focused on the ministry of individual elders to members in their districts. In Part 4 we will consider the organizational side of church life: how the elders, working together as consistory and council, assist the congregation's ministry in its various forms.

Is the institutional work of the elders less spiritual and less personal than the work they do individually among the members? Not at all. The goal is the same: to establish people in Christ. Church life functions best when sound organizational policies and practices are in place.

Note again that I'm using the word "consistory" for the assembly of elders and minister(s), as it is used in the Church Order. The "council" consists of the elders, minister(s), and deacons. On the following pages, when advice is given for the council, it also holds true for the consistory.

Part 4

38. The Council

Now that you have been ordained as an elder, you belong to a remarkable institution: the church council. No other institution in society is quite like it, because the church and its government are unique.

The council is the regulatory body in your church, yet there is nothing absolute about its power and authority. The officebearers serve in subjection to Christ, the Head of the church. They exercise their office not so much by governing as by guiding and enabling, or, better still, by serving. They follow the example of Christ, who said of himself that he came to serve rather than to be served (Matt. 20:24-28; John 13:1-17).

The council recognizes that the church members themselves are officebearers. They assume the office of believer and share in the anointing of Christ individually and corporately (Ex. 19:6; Gal. 6:2; 1 Pet. 2:5-10; 4:10; Heidelberg Catechism, Lord's Day 12). So the council will respect the mature judgment of the congregation and consult with the members on important issues. But that does not make the church a democracy.

The council decides matters on behalf of the membership, being responsible to Jesus Christ, the Head of the church. That's why prayer is important for officebearers. It is through prayer that their hearts are open to the voice of the Holy Spirit. The Spirit gives them discernment to see the needs and the possibilities in others, young and old. The Spirit enables the church to follow where Christ leads. The Holy Spirit reminds the officebearers and the members that they are part of the body of Christ.

Though elders, deacons, and pastors are ordained to different functions, they are equal "in dignity and honor" (Church Order, Art. 2). In your council there is no place for a CEO. A firm principle of the Christian Reformed Church's Church Order is that officebearers work and decide collegially and by consensus whenever possible.

The fundamental differences between the church and other institutions are summarized in Article 1 of the Church Order:

The Christian Reformed Church, confessing its complete subjection to the Word of God and the Reformed creeds as a true interpretation of this Word, acknowledging Christ as the only Head of his church, and desiring to honor the apostolic injunction that in the churches all things are to be done decently and in order (1 Cor. 14:40), regulates its ecclesiastical organization and activities in the following articles.

There are fundamental differences between being a congregation of Christ and a for-profit business: norms, practices, authority structures, and goals are unique for each. But that does not mean that church leaders should not understand themselves as accountable for the most prudent use of time and resources. They are also accountable for setting and accomplishing goals in keeping with the reason for their church's being.

Your council works toward one ultimate goal: that the body of believers will grow both in faith and in numbers. Some of that growth can be observed, perhaps even measured, but much of it only God can measure. The "product" of your work often remains invisible. You leave it to the Lord to determine how cost-effective your investment as an elder really is.

It Takes Getting Used To

I accepted my appointment as an elder with some fear. I felt I was too young and too inexperienced.

My first meeting with the council was not helpful. I had not realized that church life depends on so many arrangements that the council had to make. Some of them were matters of common sense. But my fellow officebearers debated them at great length. Even minor matters were hotly contested. I also had expected the tone of the discussions to be more spiritual and the atmosphere more devout. One elder said some unkind things to a deacon, and I felt some tension. And that first meeting was too long to suit me.

But now that I have been an elder for some time, I have grown in appreciation for what the council does. I have discovered that my fellow servants love the congregation and that some of the decisions are better for the lengthy discussions that went into their acceptance. I still think that some of my colleagues talk too much and that the chairman of council should keep the discussion more on target, but I realize that I have become a member of a body of people who seek to do God's will. I find that a great honor. I feel humble for such a task.

—*Elder Peter*

39. Using the Church Order

The Deliberative Assembly

The very existence of the Church Order assumes that the council is a deliberative body. Officebearers trust that Christ leads and guides his church. Trusting the Lord, they need not hurry. They listen to each other. They learn from each other. That is the "process" that leads to agreement or consensus. Decisions must be good and wise, but also timely. Not everyone may be ready to proceed along a new path. It's always worthwhile to seek to bring everybody "on board." That may take a lot of discussion. And discussions take time. But such investments come with rewards.

Your church is structured according to biblical standards. The council must see to it that the church remains true to the Word of God in its faith, practice, and organization. Your church, however, also faces many challenges that were unknown to the writers of the New Testament. The Bible does not address every specific situation we face today.

Many of its policies and practices are guided by the Church Order of the Christian Reformed Church in North America. It is a venerable, time-tested document from which the denomination and its individual congregations have richly profited. Its roots lie in the church order drafted by the churches of the Reformation in Europe in the sixteenth century.

Our present Church Order reflects what we believe the Word of God mandates the church to be and to do. That is especially true of things essential to church government, but the Church Order also spells out provisions for the church that are circumstantial and situational. These provisions were made by common consent for which no immediate biblical grounds could be claimed. That's why through the years, as new needs and challenges arise, the Church Order is revised to serve the churches more effectively.

You will profit greatly from consulting the Church Order and following its procedures. It will deepen your appreciation for what the church of Christ is and how it can best do its ministry. Discord in church life often stems from a misunderstanding of procedural rules agreed upon by all.

40. Structuring the Council

A Time-Honored Arrangement

In the past, Christian Reformed church councils functioned effectively with a simple structure. The minister served as president and chaired the monthly meeting; an elder was elected clerk and kept the minutes; a vice-president, or vice-all, took over when needed; and a treasurer took care of finances. The volume of business was usually such that a single monthly meeting was sufficient.

These monthly meetings were interspersed with separate elders' meetings (the consistory) and deacons' meetings.

Through the years, as councils had to deal with more diverse needs and more ambitious programs, the council's officers began to meet as an executive committee. Many councils now have this arrangement. The executive committee serves the full council in a number of ways: by preparing the council agenda, by researching upcoming agenda items, and by performing routine council duties between meetings.

Many congregations also find it helpful for an elder or deacon to serve as the elected chair of council. This means the pastor is free to participate in the meeting, and it makes use of the leadership gifts of other members.

A Revised Structure

Since the 1980s, councils have found that officebearers have less discretionary time than did their colleagues of a generation ago. As the demands of leadership steadily increased, councils in some medium-sized and larger congregations now divide their concerns over two broad areas:

▶ the regular congregational program.

▶ the pastoral needs of the membership.

To serve in the first area, congregations choose *administrative elders* and *administrative deacons*. To serve in the second area they choose *shepherding elders* and *service deacons*. (Note that the terminology for these positions varies from one congregation to another.) This type of structure may enable medium-sized and larger congregations to utilize their officebearers according to their gifts.

For example, in one common scenario the administrative elders and the administrative deacons, along with the minister or ministers, form the *administrative board*. It acts on all matters consistent with budget policies and programs approved by the full council, oversees the support staff, provides leadership to help the church respond to various challenges, makes budget proposals, and so on. This board meets monthly.

The *shepherding elders* bring pastoral care to the membership: their main task is visiting families and individual members, visiting the sick, participating in prayer ministries, encouraging the evangelism teams, overseeing the preaching and teaching ministries of the church, and so on. They meet monthly.

The *service deacons* respond to the members' long- and short-term physical needs, always in the awareness that they represent the Savior in his mercy. They also develop ministries of mercy and justice in the community and beyond, determine which causes to support, promote Christian stewardship, arrange for support of Christian education, make food pantries and other such ministries available for the community, and so on. They meet monthly.

All the officebearers meet as a *full council* three or four times a year, mostly for policy and direction setting, budget reviews, council nominations, and so on. At this meeting a comprehensive review is also conducted of the ministry of the various types of officebearers.

As an addition to this refined structure, councils sometimes create *ministry teams* to facilitate various ministries such as worship, congregational life, visiting, youth, outreach, community services, education, and so on. The administrative board may appoint team leaders for each. These leaders report periodically to the appropriate board, the consistory, or the council.

Are these developments in harmony with what we understand Reformed church governance to be? Though the Church Order does not specifically sanction this type of structure, it certainly does not contradict the spirit of the Church Order.

It is important that all the officebearers, as well as the congregation, understand the council's structure. Officebearers must know what is expected of them, and church members must know how the congregation is being led.

Advantages and Disadvantages of this Revised Structure

There are some obvious advantages to the structure outlined above. Elders and deacons have different gifts. This enables councils to nominate prospective officebearers with the gifts, skills, and interests that best suit the capacity in which they might serve. A more nimble structure with fewer people involved in decision making may help leaders respond more quickly to needs and challenges. This structure also may reduce the number of meetings individual officebearers attend.

There may also be disadvantages to this structure. Increasingly, officebearers deal with only a segment of the church's overall ministry. If a member approaches an elder or deacon with a question or even a misgiving, the elder or deacon may not know how to answer, or may not even be aware of the situation to which the member refers. Such situations are potentially embarrassing and may promote distrust in the congregation's leaders because the congregation may feel underrepresented in the governance of their church.

The preceding paragraph points to the great need for effective and careful communication. Reports of various meetings need to be sent to other officebearers in a timely manner. Background information for various decisions must be spelled out carefully. The whole council should review what the other groups have done (see also section 52). (For more on structures that enhance congregational ministry and mission, see *Healthy Churches: Missional Structures for Today*, by Dan Ackerman, Faith Alive Christian Resources.)

Synod 1973 reminded councils of their freedom to make stewardly arrangements in keeping with local needs and conditions:

> "Because the Scriptures do not present a definitive, exhaustive description of the particular ministries of the church, and because these particular ministries as described in Scripture are functional in character, the Bible leaves room for the church to adapt or modify its particular ministries in order to carry out effectively its service to Christ and for Christ in all circumstances" (*Acts of Synod*, p. 64).

41. Preparing the Agenda

The most common reason for unsuccessful council meetings is lack of preparation. Thinking through the agenda is imperative. It is wise for councils to appoint a team to draft the agenda of the upcoming meeting. In many churches this task falls to the executive committee.

Sample Agenda Process
Here's how the team of one church council worked:

▶ The team reviewed the minutes of the previous two meetings to determine two things: (1) Were previous decisions implemented and acted upon? (2) Are there any unresolved problems or unfinished business? The team considered how to facilitate action on these items and suggested solutions for the council to consider.

▶ Next, the team considered the matters that the clerk had received for the upcoming council and drafted advice for how the council might deal with them. Here are some examples:

Elder A. has a misgiving that he wants to air before the council. The team, however, advises that the elder first speak to the committee in charge of matters related to the elder's concern. One of the team members contacts the elder later and he agrees to do that.

Deacon B. has submitted a proposal about which she feels deeply. The team advises her to first seek the input of the other deacons before putting the proposal on the agenda.

Elder C. has a number of suggestions for improving the worship services. The team discusses with him the possibility of first consulting with the Worship Committee.

Elder D. has presented a proposal that the team recognizes as significant for the church's outreach program. The team agrees to place it on the agenda but secures Elder D.'s agreement to first meet with the Evangelism Committee about it and see whether further research can be done. If need be, the council can take the matter up at a following meeting.

Deacon E. directed an inquiry to the council about a deep concern. The team points out to her that council dealt with the matter the previous year and gives her a copy of the minutes. The deacon responded with a note of appreciation but requests that mention be made of her concern. The team agrees and places an informative item on the agenda.

Elder F. has requested permission for a service he wishes to perform. The team explains that for such a service no council permission is needed and encourages the elder to go ahead. They place the matter on the agenda as an informative item.

Mrs. H. has submitted a proposal to change the time of the second service. Since the matter comes through appropriate channels, the team places it on the agenda and offers a proposed process for consideration and enactment.

The Building and Grounds Committee submits a report of its monthly activities. The team places it on the agenda. One of the committee's proposals needs background, and the committee promises to supply that at the council meeting.

The team also places the deacons' report on the agenda, together with a proposal regarding an extra offering.

▶ The team also sorted through the correspondence that had come in during the previous month. The team drafted a brief report of it for the council. The mail easily fell into several categories: some items had already been responded to by the minister and the clerk of council; some were to be forwarded to the deacons and/or standing committees; some were to be received for information; and some needed council's attention.

▶ The team distributed the agenda to the officebearers a week before the meeting date, asking the officebearers to study the agenda carefully.

▶ The team also reminded the council that some elders and deacons had submitted their items too late. Normally this would mean that such items be placed on the agenda of the next meeting.

It was understood by council that the team did not serve as the final arbiter of what the assembly would consider or not. The team briefly reported every item considered. Council thankfully realized that the work of the team saved the council considerable time and that more justice was done to matters needing the officebearers' attention.

42. Conducting the Church Council Meeting

Most officebearers have come home weary after a meeting that was long on discussion and short on accomplishment. Consider these suggestions for conducting an effective meeting:

A Well-Prepared Agenda

Endless discussions often result from lack of good preparation. Officebearers intuitively sense whether a proposal has been carefully thought through, whether its ramifications have been understood, and whether its benefits are promising. Council leaders should insist that proposals be well-researched and clearly stated before they reach the council (or body of elders or deacons).

▶ The chair may remind the council members that the council is both a deliberative and a decision-making body. The discussion will remain on track when focused on the matter at hand. Decisions are most helpful when carefully considered.

▶ The chair should feel free to graciously interrupt a freewheeling discussion and suggest that the focus return to the matter before the assembly.

▶ When speakers repeat themselves or repeat what others have said, the chair should not hesitate to remind them gently that good arguments need not be stated often.

▶ When the council is divided and both sides feel deeply about the issue at hand, the chair may propose postponing the matter until the next meeting. The chair may also appoint an advisory group to study the proposal and present its findings to the council at a later meeting.

▶ Many councils make it a practice to pray for each agenda item before or after the discussion and decision. When matters seem to come to an impasse, pray.

▶ When the council is divided on an important issue and a decision must be made in the same meeting, the chair should allow extra time for discussion. If no consensus emerges, the chair may suggest a short recess, after which each officebearer is invited to make a brief summary statement. Prayer may be offered before the vote is taken.

- Decisions passed by a slim majority generally will not benefit the congregation. Councils would do well to agree to reconsider a controversial matter at a subsequent meeting. Synod's procedural rules make it possible to reconsider and rescind matters decided in previous sessions.

- Long discussions and the inability to make decisions are often symptomatic of an assembly's inner division. The officebearers should honestly address such divisions. A series of informal meetings, perhaps in a retreat setting, can be a positive step when reflecting on the nature and task of the church and the needs of the local congregation. Outside advisers may be invited to provide guidance and counsel (see section 62).

- The leaders of the council should be concerned about the interpersonal relationships of the officebearers. When relationships are strained or broken, meetings invariably become unproductive. The leaders should not hesitate to discuss with the parties concerned the need for reconciliation and offer their assistance in mediation efforts (see section 56).

Church leadership is unique; it is distinct from leadership in the spheres of business, industry, education, and state. But some principles and "best practices" used in those arenas can be helpful for the way the church conducts its affairs. Church organizations should meet their responsibilities efficiently, effectively, and purposefully. Human and material resources should be employed with utmost responsibility. And though we depend on the Holy Spirit to give the increase, we must not be averse to measuring results.

Helpful Rules of Order

Does your council use proper rules of order? It is important to do so. These rules can enable a fair discussion of issues while not allowing certain members to dominate. The Rules for Synodical Procedure or Robert's Rules of Order, though not applicable to council meetings in every respect, can be a helpful resource. Some councils may not ordinarily follow rules of order, preferring freer discussion, but will use them by mutual consent when they are deemed to be helpful.

43. Loyalty

As an elder you are both an individual with your own convictions and a member of a body of officebearers. It is important that you grow in esteem for that body. In your interactions with church members you will inevitably reflect some of your feelings for the consistory and council. Here are some things to consider:

▶ Your council deserves a good reputation in your church. Without it, your council cannot provide effective leadership. Be sure to do your share in guarding and upholding that good reputation. Your council is not perfect. If you have criticisms, bring them to the council, not to the congregation. The council's own conduct should be a source of inspiration and goodwill for the congregation.

▶ You represent the council. When a council has adopted a proposal, all council members must support it and cooperate toward its implementation. Even if you were one of the elders who voted against a proposal, you should own the decision and support it before members of the congregation.

▶ Article 29 of the Church Order stipulates that "decisions of the assemblies shall be considered settled and binding" unless it is proved that they conflict with the Word of God or the Church Order. If you feel that a decision of your council is in conflict with the Word of God or the Church Order, you have the right of appeal to your council. If that brings no resolution, you may appeal to classis, and, if necessary, to synod. If you choose that route, use utmost discretion in discussing your views with fellow church members. To preserve unity, never try to promote your divergent views outside the structure of appeal.

▶ Your council does not work in secrecy. The congregation is entitled to know what the council decides and why. Members are also entitled to understand the general substance of discussions, but not specifically who said what, how it was said, whose names were mentioned, who voted for or against specific motions, or other personal details. The council should report its actions in the church bulletin or other appropriate place, ensuring that confidentialities are guarded. Confidentiality should especially surround the pastoral work of the elders in the consistory meetings (*Acts of Synod 1991*, p. 723).

44. Electing Council Members

Isn't it a small miracle that you are an elder? From the many names the council considered and discussed, yours was put on the slate of nominees submitted to the congregation. In the intervening time the congregation raised no objections against your nomination. Then you were elected. Subsequently, the council appointed you, and you were installed in the office of elder. Now you yourself are part of the process through which the council's ranks are replenished.

Here are some important steps in the process of nominating new elders and deacons:

▶ Involve the congregation from the start. Your council may solicit names from the congregation and also invite committees to suggest names. In fact, Article 4b of the Church Order stipulates this.

▶ Part of the nominating process is "discussing names" in the council meeting. The chair may remind the officebearers that they must be honest and open, but also that information regarding those considered for office must relate to their suitability for office only. None of the information should be accusatory. It should be clearly understood that the entire discussion remains strictly confidential.

▶ What criteria do we use in nominating members to the office of elder? From 1 Timothy 3:1-7 and Titus 1:5-9 we learn that prospective candidates must be good and godly people, mature and reputable, wise and responsible. The candidates for this office should have stewardly gifts so they can "keep watch over . . . all the flock . . . [and] be shepherds of the church of God" (Acts 20:28). They must "desire" the office (1 Tim. 3:1). Though not every elder can be expected to be a gifted teacher, Scripture requires that elders be "able to teach" (1 Tim. 3:2).

▶ At what point should the nominees be informed of their nomination? Some councils secure the permission of the prospective candidates before presenting their names to the congregation. The advantage is that, should certain candidates not be able or willing to serve, their names can be deleted before being publicly announced. The disadvantage is that some decline a bit too readily since they have not yet been nominated.

For that reason other councils announce the full slate and place the responsibility on the nominees to decline with the awareness of the entire congregation. Such candidates are then under more pressure to provide good reasons for their unavailability. On balance, its seems wisest to consult with candidates before making the final list, as that approach is more sensitive to the dignity of the candidates.

▶ Church Order Article 4a states, "In calling and electing to an office, the council shall ordinarily present to the congregation a nomination of at least twice the number to be elected. When the council submits a nomination which totals less than twice the number to be elected, it shall give reasons for doing so." One such reason is that not enough qualified candidates were found. Announcing this to the congregation may stimulate a more concerted effort to develop new leaders. It may also provide an opportunity for the council to discuss other possible reasons for the lack of candidates.

▶ Normally, a council will submit one list from which the congregation elects half (or more) of the names. However, in more recent years councils have felt the need to present "double nominations," or a set of two names from which the congregation selects one. The council may, for instance, nominate two members with gifts for youth ministry and then place them as a duo on the ballot. Because some congregations may be spread out geographically, the council may draft duos of members living in specific districts. The council may also wish various age groups to be represented and hence draw up duos of candidates of similar ages. Some spiritually mature members are repeatedly not elected to office. Councils then may put two such people on a duo. (See also *Acts of Synod 1983*.)

▶ Synod opened the office of deacon to women in 1984 (*Acts of Synod 1984*, pp. 654-655). Synod 1996 made provision for women serving as elders (*Acts of Synod 1996*, pp. 550-551). Should your council wish to nominate women to the office of elder for the first time, it may be wise to gauge the readiness of the congregation. Some well-led congregational discussion may be helpful. If women are nominated and you know that many in your congregation oppose this, your council may wish to consider "double nominations" as described in the previous paragraph.

▶ Note that the Church Order stipulates that elections shall take place at a regular congregational meeting under supervision of the council. Also, the right to vote is limited to confessing members in good standing (see Art. 4c and Art. 37).

- In large congregations, or congregations that are geographically spread out, it is important that council provide a profile of the candidates nominated for office and that they be introduced to the congregation.

- The names of those elected are ordinarily announced to the congregation on the two Sundays prior to installation. Installation takes place in a worship service with the use of the appropriate form (see Church Order, Art. 4d). Synod adopted a form that distinguished between "ordination"—the ceremony in which any officebearer is brought into office for the first time, and "installation"—the ceremony in which the induction is for a subsequent term. (See *Acts of Synod 1983*, p. 643.)

- How long should an elder's term be? Most elders serve a term of three years, usually with the understanding that they can be nominated again after a leave of one or two years. Some churches have two-year terms. That may be too short in view of the fact that it probably takes nearly a year for elders to get to know the members of their districts. Article 25a of the Church Order allows for immediate eligibility for reelection if "circumstances and the profit of the church" make that advisable. "Elders and deacons who are thus reelected shall be reinstalled."

- Synod stated that laying on of hands is appropriate for the ordination/installation of all four church offices, but added that the actual laying on of hands is to be performed by ministers and elders (*Acts of Synod 1983*, p. 643). Some churches have afforded deacons and ministry associates the same privilege.

- Some councils provide training for officebearers well before nomination time; others offer it to newly appointed officebearers. In any case, training will bear much fruit.

By Lot?

Is it a good practice to select officebearers by lot? Synod 1985 did not favor the idea. It stated that "the use of the lot limits the responsibility of the office of the believer" and that "at the moment of choice [the member] is merely an observer" rather than a participant (*Acts of Synod 1985*, p. 714). Synod 1989 confirmed that judgment (*Acts of Synod 1989*, p. 500-502). Some churches use a combination of the regular election process and the casting of lots. The congregation elects twice the number of names needed. The lot is then cast, selecting half of the candidates for appointment to their respective offices. When this process is used, those who are not selected need not feel rejected by the membership.

45. Discretion and Confidentiality

It is important for elders and all officebearers to be discreet. It should become second nature for you to never discuss with third parties information your people have entrusted to you. The form for the Ordination of Elders and Deacons contains these phrases: " . . . keeping in confidence those matters entrusted to them" and "hold in trust all sensitive matters confided to you."

Councils should discourage officebearers from mentioning personal details of parishioners' lives in full meetings. This holds also for consistory meetings when elders report on home/family/pastoral visits. Exceptions may be made when the information must be relayed for the parishioners' spiritual well-being, or if their permission has been given to do so. Even then a good check would be to ask this question: "How would this parishioner feel if he or she heard me make these statements?"

More recently the matter of confidentiality has become laden with legal implications. In this litigious age people will not hesitate to sue when they feel betrayed by someone in the helping professions, even the church.

Synod drafted important guidelines for councils. The report titled "Statutes, Rules, and Laws Related to Privileged Communication to the Clergy," containing statutory references as of 1987, is available from the office of the General Secretary (*Acts of Synod 1991*, pp. 723 and 769). Following is a summary:

1. Whatever parishioners tell you in confidence is privileged communication and is to be held inviolate by you. There are two exceptions:

- if the confidential matter can bring serious harm to the one who told you or to others.

- if the person who told you gives you permission to alert the proper authorities.

Should a member share a difficult problem with you in confidence and you feel the need for competent advice, you may go to a specialist and lay out the problem while safeguarding the identity of the member. You may also tell the member that you are unable to help and suggest strongly that he or she seek the aid of a specialist.

2. The classical church visitors must make sure that local officebearers are aware of the need to protect confidential information.

3. Recognized church officials have the right to refuse to testify in court as a matter of conscience regarding confidential information received in the performance of their duty.

4. Councils must be very circumspect in processing cases of church discipline. In making public announcements, the sin of the offending member should not be mentioned. State only that the member has not repented. Consistories would do well to seek legal counsel in complicated and protracted discipline procedures.

Synod also advised every church to state "its membership requirements very clearly, including the expectation that all members are to participate in and be subject to the admonition and discipline of the church" (*Acts of Synod 1991*, p. 723). Churches, in other words, must make it plain to their members that possible disciplinary steps are part of the conditions of membership.

46. The Congregational Meeting

Part of Council

Note that the Church Order recognizes three ecclesiastical assemblies: council, classis, and synod. The congregational meeting is not one of those assemblies (Church Order, Art. 26). Rather the congregational meeting, technically, is a council meeting at which the congregation is invited to express its ideas.

Councils cannot govern constructively unless they maintain close contact with the congregation. Wise councils regularly consult with the membership through congregational meetings. Thus, the congregation has a significant share in the overall planning and administration of congregational life.

While Article 37 of the Church Order stipulates that the council shall "invite [the congregation's] judgment about . . . major matters" and that "full consideration shall be given to the judgment expressed by the congregation," it concludes by affirming that "the authority for making and carrying out final decisions remains with the council as the governing body of the church."

Christ is the Head of the body of believers—the church. The officebearers rule in his authority, so they have the final responsibility for decisions made. But they also recognize that the membership consists of mature believers (who hold "the office of all believers") whose judgment is valuable in the governance process.

A Few Observations

▶ Congregational meetings must be held "at least annually" (Art. 37), but wise councils will arrange for several a year.

▶ All professing members in good standing who are at least eighteen years old have voting privileges. That's why the meeting must be announced clearly, publicly, and well ahead of time.

▶ Congregational meetings are conducted by the council. The president of council will normally chair the meeting and assume responsibility for conducting proceedings in an orderly and constructive way. (Note that Canadian law now insists that the whole membership must approve the budget. From the government's viewpoint, the members make the final decision, not the council.)

▶ According to Article 37, "only matters which [the council] presents shall be considered." This is an important point. A congregational meeting is called by council to consider matters that it has given due consideration. Every member has the right to bring a matter before council for consideration. A member may even ask the council to address a certain matter in a congregational meeting. It is up to council, however, to decide whether it will be placed on the agenda. Members should feel free to contact the council at any time with matters of concern. In some churches the meeting customarily concludes with the chair asking, "Does anyone have any further business?" In keeping with the spirit of Article 37, such a question should be omitted.

▶ Excluded from discussion in congregational meetings are matters "which pertain to the supervision and discipline of the congregation" (Art. 37). Individual members can be sure that the personal ministry of the elders and pastors will never be divulged in a congregational meeting.

▶ Proposals adopted at a congregational meeting must be considered and adopted by the council at its subsequent meeting before they are implemented. These actions should be communicated to the congregation. In the rare instance that council may be unwilling or unable to implement a proposal passed at a congregational meeting, it will arrange for another congregational meeting at which explanation is made and further advice sought. The council must also ascertain if its desires contradict the congregation's articles of incorporation in order to avoid unnecessary legal action.

▶ A growing number of councils successfully use a less formal setting for consulting the congregation. Names such as "town hall meeting" or "congregational forum" are used for these get-togethers. They are suitable settings to update the congregation on the church's ministry program and to seek the congregation's response to its planning and visioning.

47. Searching for the Next Pastor

Exit Interview

Before your pastor leaves, make sure that you conduct an exit interview with him or her. Inform the pastor well ahead of time. Your council may wish to draft a set of questions which it would want to discuss. It would be proper that part or all of the council be present, and part or all of the search committee, but the parting pastor should be given a choice as to the size and makeup of the group.

The pastor may give valuable advice as you together evaluate the years of ministry that now come to a conclusion. Needs, possibilities, and challenges may be carefully considered. In rare cases this may also be the setting in which conflicts and misunderstandings can be resolved.

Your pastor accepted a call, you arranged a splendid farewell, and now you are without a pastor. Your church is "vacant"—an inelegant expression, since Christ's church is never vacant of Spirit-gifted leadership and care.

Rather than hurrying the calling process, the church should take time to evaluate its present situation and determine its future course. This is especially true if the parting pastor has served the congregation for a long time. The congregation needs time to adjust to (and in many cases, grieve) the pastor's parting.

Calling a New Pastor

▶ Councils should give strong considerations to hiring an interim pastor for at least several months to help lead the congregation through the process, as well as to provide ongoing pastoral service. A number of trained interim pastors are available for service in congregations for varying lengths of time. Consultation with the Classical Regional Pastor or the Office of Pastor-Church Relations can give advice as to the availability of interim personnel.

▶ Council should appoint a search committee of ten to twelve members. At least one member should be an elder and one a deacon. Special care should be taken to involve the various age and interest sectors of the congregation. The council also appoints a chairperson and preferably two secretaries: one for keeping records and one for correspondence.

▶ The committee is in a good position to weigh the situation and provide leadership. A series of consultations should be held with the council and the congregation. Congregational questionnaires and research papers may facilitate this process. All this will help the congregation to decide on the type of gifts and interests the next pastor will need, and it will help the pastors with whom the committee negotiates to decide whether they are right for the job.

▶ Your fellow congregations are connected with your search activities; we are a denominational family, and our ministers are important family members. Your choice will affect the church at large, even if only minimally. That's why the Church Order stipulates that the classis of which you are part appoint a "counselor," a pastor of one of the nearby churches, to advise your search committee and congregation (Art. 9). Synod has also stipulated that the counselor sign the letter of call which you decide to send to the pastor of your choice. Be sure to invite the counselor to the appropriate meetings of the search committee and council.

▶ Increasingly, anticipating a longer search process, congregations employ an interim pastor to serve until a new one is called. There are some pastors for whom this is a special calling, and others who serve in this capacity after retirement from regular service in congregations. In any case, it is wise that an interim be trained in this specialized ministry in order to properly lead the congregation through this challenging time.

▶ From its surveys and studies, the search committee will prepare a comprehensive statement on vision, plans, and goals for the ministry of the church. This document will also help the committee draft a job description for the new pastor. The committee should seek the support of the council at every point.

▶ The search committee should contact the Ministerial Information Service (MIS) in the Pastor-Church Relations office for a Church Profile questionnaire. Completing this form will help the committee to determine what kind of pastor the congregation needs. The studies mentioned above provide good input. The committee also should consult with the congregation and the council. The completed Church Profile should be returned to MIS.

- The committee also prepares an information packet for the use of pastors who will be contacted. The packet should contain the statement of the congregation's vision, plans, and goals, as well as material describing the congregation and surrounding community. Some churches also include a questionnaire for the potential pastor's use. The committee may also wish to enclose a copy of their church's MIS Church Profile.

- Drawing up a list of names of pastors to consider may be difficult. Sources of names include committee members, the classical counselor, council members, and the congregation. MIS can provide names of pastors with matching profiles who may be able to consider a call. The committee should also place an ad in *The Banner*.

- The committee's correspondence secretary should send an information packet to the pastors on the committee's list and those who responded to the *Banner* ad. Individualized cover letters invite them to be part of the search process.

- Committees should give the matter of confidentiality due attention. Names of pastors considered by the committee *should not be divulged* to the congregation *unless* the pastors have given their permission.

- The committee studies and evaluates the responses, checks references, conducts telephone interviews, perhaps listens to sermon tapes or videos, and reduces the long list to a short list. The committee may ask MIS for ministerial profiles of those on the short list of five or so pastors. In consultation with the council, these prospects may be invited for personal interviews and possibly for preaching. The church reimburses pastors for expenses incurred during such a visit.

- The council considers the committee's recommendation and prepares the nomination. Article 4 of the Church Order stipulates that more than one name is to be placed on the nomination, but this rule is not absolute. The article adds that if the council presents only a single nomination, it "shall give reasons for doing so." The advantage of a plural nomination is that the congregation has some choice and will feel more recognized in the process. The trend, however, is now definitely toward single nominations. Search committees put more work into the calling challenge, and explorations often lead to some assurances of interest on the part of a prospective pastor that make acceptance of the call likely.

- The search committee, in consultation with the council, is in a good position to review the salary arrangement for the new pastor. Is the proposed salary adequate? Does the new pastor seem happy with it? Have moving expenses been considered? Has the new pastor incurred other miscellaneous expenses? If there is a parsonage, is it in good repair? Does the new pastor wish to receive a housing allowance instead of occupying the parsonage? Must budget adjustments be made?

▶ Throughout the entire process the committee keeps the council and congregation informed and seeks their input. The committee must also maintain communication with the pastor(s) with whom they have had discussions. When a decision is delayed, inform the pastor(s) of that fact. It is annoying for pastors not to know whether they are still on your list or not. As soon as a pastor is no longer under consideration, he or she must be notified. The committee should express its appreciation for the fact that the pastor was willing to consider the call.

▶ The council sets the date for a congregational meeting and communicates that date clearly to the congregation. The committee provides profiles of each nominee to the members. The committee seeks the advice of the classical counselor and makes sure to have the counselor co-sign the letter of call.

48. Accountability and Encouragement

The designation "overseer" comes from Acts 20:28: "Keep watch over yourselves and all the flock of which the Holy Spirit has made you overseers. Be shepherds of the church of God."

First Peter 5:2 confirms it: "Be shepherds of God's flock that is under your care, serving as overseers."

The Christian congregation is not a democracy. Elders act in the authority of Christ. But they are servant leaders. They are shepherds, the Bible says, and they function in an atmosphere of mutual accountability. They can only do this by also encouraging one another. Good relationships among officebearers are very important. Relationships must be cultivated and tended with care.

Elders Relating to Other Elders

You are in it together—you and your fellow elders. You are each other's good resources. To be each other's "overseers" means to be concerned for each other and to take an interest in each other, expressing that concern and interest in words of appreciation and graceful gestures. Pray for your colleagues. Make prayer prominent in your meetings. Inquire about each other's well-being. Seek your fellow elders' advice. Your discussions will sometimes be marked by disagreements. Always let your relationships be blessed by assurances of acceptance and appreciation. In this culture of affirmation you can seek and express advice and you may even slip in a gentle correction.

Elders Relating to the Pastor(s)

Elders are also mandated to oversee the life and doctrine of the pastor(s). But the "Charge to the Elders" in the form for the Ordination of Elders and Deacons connects that closely with encouragement. It says: "Be wise counselors who support and strengthen the pastor." Only in the spirit of good fellowship can you hold your pastor(s) to high standards of excellence. Dwell on the positive aspects of the gifts and ministry of your pastor(s). Try to foster a climate of openness and acceptance. (See 2 Thess. 2:13-17.)

The most important part of the pastor's task is the ministry of the Word and sacraments. The elders must see to it that the pastor is given ample time to prepare sermons. Preaching should be discussed now and then with the pastor(s) and always in a nonthreatening and nonjudgmental way. Pastors will appreciate helpful suggestions and hints. You should consider together whether sermons are balanced and relevant, are presented in an engaging manner, and give evidence of careful preparation. But above all, you need to ask, *Is Christ preached?*

Many councils appoint a small committee (or perhaps designate the executive committee) to which the pastor reports regarding matters of ministry and preaching. This is also a good setting for consultation, suggestions, and feedback. (See also section 49.)

Elders Relating to Parishioners

The elders must also oversee the congregation. Article 12a of the Church Order states, "[The pastor], with the elders, shall supervise the congregation." Article 25b is more detailed:

> "The elders, with the minister(s), shall oversee the doctrine and life of the members of the congregation and fellow officebearers, shall exercise admonition and discipline along with pastoral care in the congregation, shall participate in and promote evangelism, and shall defend the faith."

The form for the Ordination of Elders and Deacons spells out similar details: "Elders are thus responsible for the spiritual well-being of God's people. They must provide true preaching and teaching . . . and faithful counsel and discipline. . . . And they must promote fellowship and hospitality among believers, ensure good order in the church, and stimulate witness to all people."

The supervisory task of the elders extends also over the programmatic side of church life. The elders are responsible for maintaining and improving such organized activities as worship services, education classes, evangelism, and so on. One important and welcome development in many congregations is the formation of small groups. While they offer great opportunities for spiritual growth, ministry, and service, they also have pitfalls. Leaders may be

A Unique Nature

Congregations are known for their climate, their mood, their spirit, and their atmosphere. Congregations have a soul. Elders can contribute toward a quality of grace and goodness in a congregation. By cultivating their own personal love and hope for their congregation, they will be able to inspire the membership to think well of their church.

untrained, or situations may develop that are beyond the ability of the members to cope. It is important that elders be aware of the formation of small groups, visit them periodically, and assist in training group leaders.

Elders should also "diligently encourage the members of the congregation to establish and maintain good Christian schools" and to actively participate in organizations and institutions that promote God's kingdom (see Art. 71 and 72).

The ordination form states clearly that the governing task of the elders is spiritually conditioned. The "Charge to the Elders" includes these words: "Remember at all times that if you would truly give spiritual leadership in the household of faith, you must be completely mastered by your Lord."

The Practice of Mutual Censure

Mutual accountability assumes a unique form in the time-honored practice of mutual censure or, as it was termed in the past, *censura morum*. Article 36b of the Church Order stipulates that councils conduct this form of mutual supervision "at least four times a year." Focus will be on "the performance of the official duties of the officebearers."

When done thoughtfully, this practice can be very helpful, especially when the officebearers seriously evaluate the quality of the council's work. It also provides a good opportunity for the council members to deal with potential problems in a spirit of love and trust.

Article 36b also implies that councils should regularly set aside time to evaluate the quality of their ministry and the well-being of the congregation. Can improvements be made? Can new initiatives be taken? Councils should also periodically thank God for the privilege of serving together as colleagues in a spirit of friendship and mutual appreciation.

Councils, then, must put on the mind of Christ and accept Paul's benediction from 2 Thessalonians 2:16-17: "May our Lord Jesus Christ himself and God our Father, who loved us and by his grace gave us eternal encouragement and good hope, encourage your hearts and strengthen you in every good deed and word."

The Practice of Signing the Form of Subscription

The Christian Reformed Church is a confessional church. That means we wish our faith experience and our life's walk to be in keeping with the confessions of the church. It is especially important that the leaders in the church know and cherish those confessions. So the practice arose that officebearers, at the time of their installation in their office, would sign a document that spells out their promises to maintain the confessions. This document is called the Form of Subscription.

At its very beginning in 1857, our denomination adopted this form essentially unchanged from its initial draft at the Synod of Dort in 1618-1619. Synod 1976 called the form a "regulatory instrument" and stated that it was meant to be "for safeguarding the administration of the Word and the government of the church in harmony with the confessions" (*Acts of Synod 1976*, p. 577).

Synod 2006 decided that the form should be revised in contemporary language and in light of the church's current understanding of what officebearers must consent to as leaders in the churches. It proposed that a revision be drafted and submitted to Synod 2008 for approval. The proposed revision was not accepted and was sent back to committee for reformulation.

Here are some key sentences from the present form that stipulate in what sense the confessions are binding on officebearers:

> "By means of our signatures [we] declare truthfully and in good conscience before the Lord that we sincerely believe that all articles and points of doctrine set forth [in these three confessions] fully agree with the Word of God."

> "We promise therefore to teach these doctrines diligently, to defend them faithfully, and not to contradict them."

> "We pledge . . . not only to reject all errors that conflict with these doctrines but also to refute them."

> "We promise in addition that if . . . the council, classis, or synod considers it proper at any time . . . to require a fuller explanation of our views . . . we are always willing and ready to comply . . . realizing that the consequences of refusal to do so is suspension from office."

Through the years there have been voices in the church that expressed difficulty with the forceful formulation of the Form of Subscription. Its language was thought by some to be "silencing," in spite of its good intent. Synod added a qualifier in response to these criticisms by stating:

"The subscriber does not by subscription to the confessions declare that these doctrines are all stated in the best possible manner or . . . cover all that the Scriptures teach on the matters confessed. Nor does the subscriber declare that every teaching of the Scriptures is set forth in our confessions."

Synod added that a subscriber is "not bound to the references, allusions, and remarks that are incidental to the formulation of these doctrines, nor to the theological deductions." (Supplement to Art. 5 of the Church Order, *Church Order and Rules for Synodical Procedure 2008*, p. 29).

In the meantime, it cannot be denied that the creeds have given our denomination a high degree of unity and a deepened insight into our identity as Christ's church. The confessions offer deeply grounded guidance to the contemporary church by linking us to the past and its many treasures. In this age of relativism that is not an unnecessary luxury.

It has also been pointed out, however, that the truths of Scripture require contemporary expression in the church's creedal message. Cultural situations are in a state of flux, and new challenges are making new formulations of responses necessary. Other parts of the worldwide church of Christ must also be recognized for their insightful readings of God's Word in today's context. Our own denomination has done commendable work by adopting the confessional statement *Our World Belongs to God: A Contemporary Testimony*.

Our Three Ecumenical Creeds:

- the Apostles' Creed (from before the fourth century)

- the Nicene Creed (from the fourth century)

- the Athanasian Creed (from around the sixth century)

Our Three Reformed Creeds ("Forms of Unity"):

- The Belgic Confession (from 1561, drafted by Guido de Bres; adopted by the Synod of Dort, 1618-1619)

- The Heidelberg Catechism (from 1563, drafted by Zacharius Ursinus and Casper Olevianus; approved by the Synod of Dort, 1618-1619)

- The Canons of Dort (adopted by the Synod of Dort, 1618-1619)

49. Supporting the Pastor(s)

Because the weight of a minister's office and the demands made on his or her time and energy are probably more than the congregation and council realize, more needs to be said about care to pastors. Here is one real-life example:

> A young member of the church was found to have used and sold drugs. The distraught parents phoned the minister, who subsequently joined a team of professional caregivers. Over the next few weeks the minister's log showed twelve visits and conferences: three with the parents, four with their son, one with the high school guidance counselor, two with the therapist who was brought in, one with a police officer, and one with a court official. The minister had to adjust his schedule several times to make some of the visits. They were emotionally draining, and the minister did not feel at liberty to inform the council of these time investments.

Is this an exceptional situation? Probably. Remember, though, that ministers regularly face exceptional situations.

How Can Elders Support Pastors?

▶ Ministers are shepherds, not simply employees of the congregation. They usually do not seek sympathy, but they value understanding and expressions of appreciation. It means a lot to ministers when elders are aware of the weight of their responsibilities.

▶ Elders and deacons should see to it that ministers' salaries are commensurate with the demands of their training and office. Compensation should be discussed annually in an atmosphere of appreciation, trust, and frankness. A helpful guide to average salaries by region called the "Pastor Compensation Survey" can be obtained from the CRC denominational office.

▶ Ministers have an open-ended job. The boundaries between private life and professional life are easily blurred. Elders can help ministers to keep the two areas distinct and can encourage the minister to live wholeheartedly in each.

▶ In view of the demands on their time and energy, ministers tend not to read, study, and reflect as much as they should. Elders should encourage and help arrange for ministers to take regular study leaves and sabbaticals, and plan time each week for reading and replenishment. Several grants are available through national organizations and foundations to help fund sabbaticals. While it is likely that the minister will take the lead in planning for a study leave, conference, or sabbatical, it's essential that he or she receive the encouragement of the elders and the whole congregation.

▶ Ministers need regular relief from preaching. Those weeks when they need not prepare sermons will be used for catching up on visiting, administration, and teaching preparation.

▶ Elders are not only shepherds to the members but also to the ministers. They should discuss with the ministers how pastoral care can best be provided for them. The ministers' spiritual and emotional health should not be taken for granted. These matters can best be discussed within a small group or within a peer group.

▶ Synod has often expressed its concern for the well-being of pastors. Synod 1982 proposed that local churches set up a small support group for each of their ministry personnel (*Acts of Synod 1982*, p. 78). Not every church or pastor has found this arrangement helpful. More helpful is the encouragement for pastors to find a "life" outside the congregation. This may take the form of an ecumenical gathering or study group of pastors in the community, a denominational peer group, or a regular spiritual guide or counselor.

▶ Article 15 of the Church Order stipulates that ministers, by way of exception, may obtain a primary or supplementary form of income. For churches that are not capable of supplying the minister with a sufficient salary, this may be a possibility to negotiate. The approval of classis is necessary.

50. Exercising Discipline

Accepting church membership means benefiting from its blessings and graces; it also means accepting the church's discipline when appropriate. As members of Christ's body we are accountable to one another and especially to those who are appointed to watch over the church. For pastors and elders this is often a very difficult part of their ministry. In one short sentence the ordination form lays out the mandate: "Be compassionate, yet firm and consistent in rebuke and discipline."

The denomination itself has tried to help the churches in this task. The entire fourth part of the Church Order (Art. 78-84) is devoted to the ministry of discipline in the church.

Discipline has one goal: to bring people back to God. Discipline is much like "discipling," which means to encourage and train people to be followers of Jesus Christ. Restoring erring members to honorable membership is part of the elders' tasks. Actually, all members are part of this work. Members assist one another in the quest for obedience, holiness, and congregational health. Fostering an atmosphere of openness and mutual accountability will help prevent incidents of formal discipline.

Discipline of Full Members

▶ Elders struggle with the question of when to proceed with formal discipline. Is every sin censurable? Potentially, yes; in practice, no. The degree to which the sin is practiced is a factor. The public nature of the offense is a factor. The attitude of the sinner is probably the biggest factor. If the offender persists, shows no repentance, and will not acknowledge the particular sin, then, after repeated pleadings, formal censure begins.

▶ A team of two elders, or an elder and a minister, visits the member and asks him or her to explain the presumed offense. They discuss the issue thoroughly, thoughtfully, and prayerfully. Should the team conclude that the conduct of the member is an offense and should the member refuse to acknowledge this, the team will inform the member that they will report the visit to the consistory and seek its counsel.

▶ If the consistory considers the offense worthy of censure, another visit will be made. Again the team will try to bring the member to acknowledge the sin and to repent of it. If they are unsuccessful, the consistory must decide whether to proceed with discipline. If it does, it will inform the member, through the visiting elders, that he or she is barred from the Lord's Supper. Other membership privileges are also suspended, such as voting at congregational meetings and holding office. None of these actions—formerly called "silent censure"—are reported to the congregation at this stage.

▶ If subsequent visits are unfruitful, the consistory must then decide whether to proceed with the next stage of censure, sometimes called "public censure."

▶ The visiting team will inform the member that an announcement will be made in an upcoming worship service that "a brother or sister of the congregation" refuses to repent of a certain sin and that the congregation will be asked to pray for him or her. This is the first step of public censure. The member remains anonymous, and the nature of the sin is not divulged.

▶ If the member remains unrepentant, the consistory will decide whether to take the second step of public censure: an announcement to the congregation that the member has not repented and will be excommunicated from the church fellowship on a predetermined date if he or she remains unrepentant.

▶ Before the consistory takes this step it must consult with classis and receive its endorsement. Also, well before the announcement is made, the visiting team will visit the member again, plead with him or her to repent, and explain the details of the step the council intends to take. If the member has no change of heart, the announcement is made on the appointed Sunday. The announcement contains a request to the congregation to pray for the member. The member's name is revealed, but the nature of the sin is not. The date of the actual excommunication is also mentioned.

▶ If possible, the team will visit again before the date of excommunication. If this is fruitless, the consistory will proceed with excommunication. The final announcement to that effect will be made to the congregation. The form for excommunication in the back of the *Psalter Hymnal* may be read.

- Excommunication does not end the obligation of the consistory and the congregation from seeking repentance and reconciliation when the person involved is open to it, and all are under obligation to continue praying for the excluded member. It's notable that after the form for excommunication there is a form for readmission.

- Be sure to keep accurate written records of all proceedings referred to above.

Be Gentle

Throughout the painful process of discipline, elders should keep in mind Paul's pointed words: "Brothers and sisters, if someone is caught in a sin, you who live by the Spirit should restore that person gently. But watch yourselves, or you also may be tempted" (Gal. 6:1).

Discipline of Baptized Members

Formal discipline of baptized members who have not made public profession of faith involves a simpler process than that of full members. When such a member neglects the life and worship of the community or falls into sinful patterns of life, the consistory, after repeated attempts to bring the person to repentance and faith, will inform the person of its intention to terminate his or her membership in the church. This process, too, should be accompanied by persistent pastoral care and fervent prayer.

When Delinquent Members Resign

In many cases those under discipline will resign their membership before the process is completed. This is a symptom of our individualistic culture and the failure of many to understand the responsibilities of membership in the church community. Breaking fellowship with the church by resignation should therefore not be accepted lightly or quickly. The elders will continue pleading earnestly with the member to return to the community. But this course of action is the member's choice and, in the end, the consistory must consider the membership terminated. The congregation shall be informed accordingly.

When Members Move Away

In this age of mobility it sometimes happens that a member moves away without informing the council regarding their church membership. In this case, the district elder should call the member and encourage him or her to make proper provisions for membership with a church of Christ near their new residence. This may have a positive or a negative result. Some members may request their membership to remain at their home church, and the consistory may consent to such an arrangement. In the absence of cooperation, however, the consistory may declare a membership lapsed after a period of two years from the date of departure.

Inherent Weaknesses

The Christian Reformed Church has always held that the established practice of church discipline is in keeping with the Scriptures but is not in every detail prescribed by Scripture. The church has held that a common agreement would bring a uniform standard to all the churches and would, by that token, add to the justice and integrity of the process.

But through the years the weaknesses of the accepted system have also become apparent. The actual instances where the full disciplinary procedure was enacted have diminished through the years. In our highly mobile, complex, and individualistic society, a system of discipline based on congregational loyalty and church authority seems almost impossible. Synod has struggled with this over the years, adding corrections and ad hoc provisions.

Synods' Nuanced Concerns

Here are some examples of how Synod has dealt with issues relating to discipline:

- The CRC has consistently made a case for Christian education. What about those who disagree? Synod 1955 said that such people should be subject only to rebuke, not to discipline.

- What about membership in "neutral" labor unions? Synod 1943 said that discipline should be applied only to those who participate in such a union's "evil practices."

- What about those who seek rebaptism? Synod 1973 said not to go beyond admonition.

- Synod 1982 stated that consistories should be careful not to single out those found to have sinned against the seventh commandment for discipline.

- In the controversy around the charismatic movement, Synod 1990 cautioned churches that all believers are children of God.

- The Form for Excommunication uses stern language. Synod 1991 said that it does not have to be read in a worship service. That same synod declared that our disciplinary system need not be "imposed" on congregations that come from different ethnic communities.

For more information, see *Acts of Synod 1961*, p. 96; *Acts of Synod 1962*, p. 401; *Acts of Synod 1976*, p. 53, 631-66; *Acts of Synod 1982*, p. 40; *Acts of Synod 1991*, pp. 263-84, 720-23.

Mentioning Names

On the one hand, synod declared that the entire congregation is to be lovingly involved in admonishing the erring brother or sister, but stipulated that in the matter of actual censure the announcement was to be done without mentioning names. The question of whether to mention names or not is very problematic. How can a local church be biblically consistent in this matter? In this litigious age the legality of stating names from the pulpit is still a matter of debate. Councils have resorted to engaging legal help.

Word Ministry, Pastoral Care, and Community

The church has two formidable weapons for good: preaching and teaching the Word of God and personal pastoral care.

All church members sin. All need forgiveness. The heart of the gospel addresses those realities: it tells of the blood of Christ, repentance, and forgiveness. Some members struggle with weaknesses that they just cannot overcome. The church assures them that they will prevail in the Lord's grace. Some members ultimately reject the Savior, and they will leave the church.

The church has one more spiritual treasure: the communion of saints. The fellowship of believers has assumed wonderful expression through small groups, household groups, prayer groups, Bible circles, and so on. But the exercise of discipline often played itself out in a setting of loneliness.

Our tradition correctly values the preaching of the pure gospel and sound doctrine. But these must always point away from themselves to the living Savior. Churches will fight the battle against sin and misconduct best in the presence and company of the living Savior.

51. Discipline of Officebearers

One of the saddest tasks that a council is ever called to perform is to discipline one of its own members: a minister, elder, deacon, or ministry associate.

Most circumstances surrounding the discipline of officebearers are complex, and councils may not know how to proceed. It is always a good idea to call in the classical church visitors for advice early in the process. When the pastor is involved, the council may turn to the denomination's office of Pastor-Church Relations. The classical regional pastor connected with Pastor-Church Relations can also serve as a valuable resource person.

Guidelines for the Discipline of Officebearers

▶ Articles 82-84 of the Church Order deal with the discipline of officebearers. Censurable offenses by officebearers are generally committed in the following areas: violations of the Form of Subscription (see section 48 of this manual), neglect or abuse of office, or serious deviations from sound doctrine and godly conduct (Art. 83).

▶ The council suspending the accused officebearer must seek the concurrence of the nearest Christian Reformed church council. If the two councils disagree, the matter goes to classis for resolution. Suspension takes effect if classis approves the first council's action.

▶ If the ensuing judicial process establishes the officebearer's guilt and if this would lead to the officebearer's genuine repentance, the council may lift the suspension. The council may also choose to depose the officebearer if it judges that the sin, even though repentance has taken place, would hamper further service. Councils can restore suspended officebearers to service only when doing so would glorify God and benefit the church (Art. 84).

▶ The deposition of a minister of the Word requires the approval of the classis of which the local church is part. Classis makes its decision with the concurring advice of the synodical deputies of the three neighboring classes. The actual deposition is done by the offending minister's council. The stated clerk of classis must inform the other classes in the denomination of the deposition, and they must each inform the clerks of the councils of their churches.

▶ When a minister resigns from office because of having fallen into some sin or while under discipline, the church council must continue the procedures as outlined in Articles 82-84 of the Church Order. In general, the council must make a disposition of the status of a minister who resigns. It must declare which of the following four conditions prevails:

1. The resigned minister is honorably released.

2. The resigned minister is released.

3. The resigned minister is dismissed.

4. The resigned minister is in the status of one deposed.

▶ When ministers, guilty of a censurable sin, resign their membership in the CRC, the formal disciplinary process is discontinued. The disposition as outlined above must then still be made.

▶ A deposed minister may make application toward readmission to office. The decision to declare such a minister eligible for a call is to be made by the classis in which the deposition took place. The concurring advice of the three synodical deputies from the neighboring classes is required (see Church Order, Art. 84).

Another Distinction

The church distinguishes between *general discipline* and *special discipline* of officebearers. General discipline applies to officebearers in their role as members of the church. Special discipline applies to them in their role as officebearers.

General discipline is not to be applied until special discipline has been initiated. When repentance has been expressed during the process of special discipline, general discipline is usually not applied, even when an officebearer is ultimately deposed from the office.

Special discipline begins with temporarily suspending officebearers from the duties and privileges of office. At this stage the officebearers have not yet been found guilty of offense. The reason for this step is that the judicial process that follows is thus not encumbered by the tasks the officebearers have pledged to do.

52. Communication

Council must assure that a well-functioning communication system is in place. Such a system provides for a smooth information flow from council to congregation and from congregation to council and, generally, keeps members informed about congregational activities.

An effective communication system doesn't just happen. It must be designed and tended. The advantages of such a system are many. Members will relate to the church better when they know what goes on, what programs are available, and what challenges have been met. They also want to know what their council is doing and why.

What Makes for Good Communication?

▶ Pastors, elders, and deacons must keep each other informed. Paul advises in Acts 20:28 to "keep watch over . . . all the flock." You should know what is going on in the congregation. Be each other's eyes and ears and share pertinent observations with the proper officebearer.

▶ The church bulletin is an effective communication device. Many churches also publish a periodic newsletter containing information on the church's programs and the individual members' well-being. The production of these media deserves the full cooperation of council members, committee secretaries, and others who contribute information. Promptness, brevity, and accuracy are always appreciated.

▶ Many churches maintain a website. Both members and those looking for a church increasingly use the Web for information and to gain a feel for the congregation. Ensuring that the church's site is attractive, informational, and timely is an effective ministry.

▶ All communication must be marked by honesty, integrity, and clarity. Oversights and inaccuracies must be promptly corrected. The congregation will benefit from knowing that good services were rendered, that good success followed, that difficulties were acknowledged, that problems were faced and some solved, that fellow members celebrated events, and also that some members shed tears.

▶ Officebearers and church members have to talk together! They must consult together, pray together, think together, explore together, encourage each other, be concerned about spiritual growth together, and be concerned about the calling of the church in the neighborhood and the world.

53. Visioning, Mission, Planning, Programming, and Goal Setting

Most members assume that certain parts of a congregation's ministry are "givens": church services are held, pastoral care is offered, classes are taught, and a variety of groups and committees meet at stated times. This has been true for generations, and it will be true for years to come. These basic elements are woven into the existence of the church. They are what the church is all about.

But in recent times, churches have begun to ask such questions as, "Who are we?" "What do we have to offer?" "Why are we here?" "What is our calling?" To answer those questions, churches are assessing their convictions, gifts, needs, interests, resources, and skills and how those characteristics fit with the needs of the congregation, the community, and the broader world. Their leaders are speaking of vision statements, mission statements, master planning, goal setting, prioritizing, self studies, congregational surveys, monitoring progress and change, and so on.

Comprehensive planning usually invites churches to go through some helpful steps.

> ▶ For example, your church may draft a *vision statement* to help the membership see more clearly who they are as a church community and what their ideals are for their place in the world.

> ▶ Then you may wish to create a *mission statement* to outline the steps you need to take to implement those spiritual ideals.

> ▶ That would involve some serious planning (sometimes called "master planning"): spelling out what you intend to do to accomplish this mission in terms of assessing available talent, interests, resources, and congregational backing.

> ▶ That, in turn, would require laying out a program of action. Interspersed in it would be *goal setting*, which enables you to stay the course, and *evaluation*, by which effectiveness and benefits of that particular ministry are clearly stated and observed.

The Council's Role

The council must take the leadership in any kind of vision process. Here are some things to consider.

- ▶ Your regional CRC Home Missions Team may have resources or personnel to guide you through the process.

- ▶ The council must be ready to set aside considerable time, effort, and prayer for the vision process and its implementation.

- ▶ The council must set a high priority on this process in order to gain congregational support.

- ▶ The council must be ready to tackle difficult issues and challenges that emerge from this process. Problem areas long swept under the rug will emerge, and dealing with them in an open and healthy way is imperative.

- ▶ Members outside the council, along with a few key council leaders and the pastoral staff, should form a task force to oversee and guide the vision process.

- ▶ The council must commit itself to implementing the vision and goals, so that the vision process does not become a waste of valuable time.

- ▶ A vision is seldom clear right away. It often takes several years of working with the goals and refining them to make it a good tool for the church's ministry.

If your church has not done any visioning studies and planning, consider doing so. The advantages are many. You will involve the members in searching the Scriptures regarding the nature and calling of the church. Members will be challenged to discover their gifts and to use them in the Lord's service. You will probably discover new gifts and talents among your members, and you will help them to discern needs in your church's neighborhood that they are equipped to meet. Most important, your church may win people for the Lord and provide them with a wonderful church home.

Balance

One of the dangers churches face is stagnation. Another is misunderstanding. The church leadership must be aware of congregational needs but also of challenges. A lively interaction between members and leaders can lead to surprising possibilities and results. Your prayerful intercession as elders can give impetus to fresh initiatives and involvement.

54. Relating to Church Staff

Almost all Christian Reformed churches employ secretarial and administrative personnel, and more than half have additional church ministry staff workers. Effective staff performance and cooperation depend on good staff provisions.

Caring for the Church Staff

▶ You have appointed your staff people for their professional skills and vision. Grant them every professional courtesy. Hold them in the highest esteem.

▶ Each staff person should have a contract agreed upon between him/her and the council. All conditions of employment should be carefully spelled out and clearly understood.

▶ Each staff person should have a job description. Job descriptions should be regularly consulted and fine-tuned as necessary.

▶ Internal staff relationships are very important. The staff should meet once a week for prayer, planning, reporting, and mutual accountability. Differences should not be allowed to remain unresolved.

▶ The pastor or another staff member should serve as staff coordinator or supervisor. This person should coordinate and integrate staff activities and be its main spokesperson to council. The staff coordinator will see to it that all major planning and decision making is done by staff consensus. No new ministry projects should be initiated without broad staff backing.

▶ Councils should appoint a small "staff subcommittee" to supervise the staff and serve as staff liaison to council.

▶ The staff should submit a written report of its work and vision to the council. This should be submitted first to the staff coordinator/supervisor and discussed with him/her. Individual staff members should be given the courtesy to attend council meetings as resource persons. When their part of the report is discussed, they should have the privilege of the floor.

▶ Communications between individual staff members and between staff and council is important. The staff coordinator will give this careful attention.

55. Dealing with Change

A vigorous church ministry almost always involves change. Change is not always welcomed by church members and leaders, but without it church life will stagnate. The early years of the sixteenth-century Reformation produced incredible growth, but believers also had to cope with profound changes. Christ does not call us to be comfortable where we are, but to follow him into his future.

The Elder's Role

▶ Change for the sake of change is unhelpful. Opposing all change is bad too. You as a council must determine, with an open mind, which changes should be accepted courageously and which should be countered. Explain your policy to the congregation.

▶ All change requires thorough preparation. Do you understand the proposed ministry that will involve substantial change? Do you have the necessary resources? Are those in charge skilled to see it through? Are the changes in keeping with the Word of God and the confessions? Has the congregation been duly prepared and informed? You can cope confidently with change if you are convinced that you are on course.

▶ Consistency is essential. Once you have agreed on a certain program and given those in charge your blessing, you cannot, as a council, go into hiding when opposition becomes vocal. Assure the congregation that the old foundations have not crumbled, but don't backpedal under pressure. Even council members who were lukewarm toward the initial plans must stand by the people who are carrying the responsibilities.

▶ Maintain a balanced program of ministry. For example, you may agree to introduce a new type of music into worship, but assure the congregation that you will continue to treasure seasoned hymnody as well. When introducing a new ministry connected with the youth of the church, review whether your ministry to the elderly could be improved as well.

▶ Monitor change. As council members and leaders, review ministry programs and practices regularly. Make corrections and adjustments as necessary.

56. Dealing with Conflict

Few churches are spared the anguish of congregational conflict. Dealing with conflict and working toward resolution is one of the hardest parts of congregational life. The issues and dynamics surrounding such conflict are usually very complex.

Unresolved conflicts grow. The longer they last, the more difficult resolution becomes. Conflicts between parties that have dug in for battle can rarely be resolved without outside help. For that reason, the following general observations will need to be augmented by competent resource people along the way.

The Conflict Resolution Process

▶ Before you get the two parties around the bargaining table, resolve that you will take only a small step at a time. Conflicts are rarely solved quickly. (If they are, they will probably flare up again.) Both parties hold deep feelings and strong perceptions; they will not yield readily. Before you can hope to resolve a conflict, you must contain it. That is a small victory.

▶ The two parties in the conflict (each of which may comprise a cluster of members) must agree to your ministry to them. It must be clearly understood that your offer of help has been accepted by everyone involved.

▶ Be charitable and sympathetic toward all the participants. They have not usually become embroiled in this conflict by bad intent. They probably feel threatened and hurt by events over which they may have had no control. If you find it difficult to like them as persons, it is because they are in bondage to fear and anger. Be patient with them. Don't allow their fear and anger to rub off on you.

▶ The preparatory stage of your efforts is important. Visit with one party at a time. Go back and forth between the two. Gently remind the parties that you are not a miracle worker and that their cooperation is a key factor in arriving at a resolution. Assure them also that if all parties earnestly seek reconciliation, they should expect that it will happen. Above all, assure the parties and commit yourself to be impartial and not to take sides.

▶ Keep careful records of all sessions and proceedings.

- As you visit with each of the parties, try to determine what the contested issues are. Do both parties give the same account? Who is involved? How high is the anger level? Is it clear what each party demands from the other? As you interview the parties, do some probing. Give them feedback. If you see inconsistencies and discrepancies, follow up on them in a nonthreatening way.

- Each party will invariably be convinced of the rightness of its cause. Each wants to come out a winner in the contest. Point out that justice is important to you, but that reconciliation can only be the result of conceding points, accepting explanations, letting go of presumed bad motives, and honoring assurances of good faith.

- Now the hard part: conduct a face-to-face meeting of the parties. If you have found during the preparatory stage that anger and hurt run very deep, you may suggest bringing in some skilled mediators. But before you do so, make sure the idea has the approval of both parties and the church council. The parties may initially oppose the idea. Point out, patiently, that they have to face reality: their conflict is serious and will do great harm to themselves, to their children, and to the congregation if it remains unresolved.

- Begin the bargaining meeting with welcome and prayer. Briefly state the purpose of the meeting. Make an appeal for everyone's goodwill and cooperation. Next, spell out the ground rules. Point out that you are in charge of the meeting. Anyone who wishes to speak must first be recognized by you. You will not allow people to interrupt each other, and common courtesy is expected of all. State also that you (and any others with you) as mediator have pledged yourself to impartiality and fairness. Explain that this is not a court session at which verdicts are laid down. This is a meeting of reconciliation at which followers of Christ strive to overcome their differences and accept one another as members of Christ's body.

- Then read a carefully prepared statement about the nature of the conflict, the issues at stake, and perhaps a summary of how the conflict developed. You may also refer to previous meetings with the individual parties.

- Invite the participants to respond. Allow ample time to go over details even though you see little progress. Keep the discussion on track. Appeal to the parties to accept each other's explanations as sincere. Do not allow anyone to ascribe bad motives to anyone else. Do not allow angry outbursts and harsh accusations, but do allow anger to surface. If there appears to be some reason for anger, ask the opposing party to respond. If the response is even remotely positive, summarize it in your own words. Try to be the catalyst for the parties to offer clarifications, explanations, and assurances of goodwill. See whether misunderstandings and misinterpretations can be removed. Solicit responses when that happens.

▶ This stage of the process is very unpredictable. Don't hesitate to announce a brief recess to consult together as mediators. If the meeting has gone well, draft a statement of explanations and conclusions, sit down with the leaders of each party separately, and see if they will agree to the statement. Then call the meeting to order again and negotiate the acceptance of the statement as a basis for resolution and reconciliation.

▶ If it appears that another session is necessary, inform the participants of this in a charitable way, impressing upon them the need to refrain from further action and talk that could set the process back.

▶ When reconciliation has been reached, a modest form of celebration can be helpful. Perhaps the parties will agree to come together, shake hands, and assure one another of goodwill and acceptance. Pray together to thank God for reconciliation.

▶ If the conflict was a public one, decide whether a statement should be made to the congregation. If you think it advisable, get the approval of the parties.

▶ Follow-up care is vital. The parties need to be visited and assured of God's grace. Ongoing expressions of fear need to be addressed in personal visits. The pastor, especially, can play a wholesome role in this effort.

57. Overseeing Worship Services

Church Order Article 52a states, "The consistory shall regulate the worship services." Worship services are at the center of the congregation's life. We gather in worship to praise our Lord and Savior and to experience our unity as God's people and Christ's body. Nothing contributes so much to congregational health and growth as preaching and worship.

Worship Service Guidelines

▶ The worship service should include preaching, sacraments, praise, prayer, and offerings.

▶ Synods generally have been concerned about preserving uniformity among the churches in liturgical practices. Article 47 of the Church Order specifies that congregations use synodically approved songs for worship (the *Psalter Hymnal*, in other words), but in practice this regulation is widely ignored. More recently, synods have recognized the need for diversity and spontaneity in worship and have allowed councils a degree of flexibility (*Acts of Synod 1970*, p. 69; *Acts of Synod 1991*, pp. 706-707, summarized in *Manual of Church Government 2008* p. 224).

▶ Worship services are to be conducted by ministers who must "explain and apply Holy Scripture" (Art. 54a). In case of "reading services" the council must approve the sermons. The Church Order states that the Heidelberg Catechism shall ordinarily be used in the preaching every Sunday (Art. 51-54).

▶ Preaching is a prominent element in the worship service. In it the Word is explained and proclaimed, the kingdom is announced, the salvation of Christ is proclaimed, and the congregation is summoned to repentance, faith, and obedience. God's people are established in their covenantal walk with God and are equipped for service. Worship is an end in itself and also a means to an end.

The Role of the Elders

▶ Preparation for worship services is most important. Many churches now have worship committees that assist in preparing the services. The pastor(s) will be part of this process. It may take extra time to work with a team rather than having the pastor plan worship solo, but all

Responsive Worship

In worship, believers meet communally before God, who is present in Word, Spirit, and grace. An extraordinary dialogue takes place: God and his children address each other and respond to each other.

Some of the acts on God's part are the reading of the Word and preaching its meaning in the life of the congregation (through a designated servant), the assurance of pardon for sin, and the blessings pronounced upon the congregation.

Some of the acts on the part of the congregation are confession of sin, prayer, singing, praise, offering, surrender, and listening and responding to the preaching.

In the sacraments God offers the assurance of his grace through water, bread, and wine, and the congregation receives these gifts in gratitude and faith.

will benefit in the end. Worship services are communal; preparations deserve to be made communally as well.

▶ Be aware of the seasons of the church year such as Epiphany, Lent, Easter, Pentecost, and Advent. The tone and mood of the services are affected by these seasons' unique focus on different aspects of God's saving work.

▶ Remember also that specific congregational experiences may call for services that range from celebration to lament.

▶ Elders, pastors, and worship committee members should develop spiritual and theological antennae to assure excellence in congregational music and singing. Helpful summaries of principles that can guide them in this endeavor can be found in the church hymnals. They deserve careful study. Church music should be biblical, catholic, confessional, and pastoral.

▶ Congregational prayer deserves careful preparation. It is a unique event in which the entire congregation assembles for supplication and intercession. Prayers should reflect the focus of the preaching and worship service, the needs and challenges of the congregation, and the needs and conditions of the world. The intercessory element should never be absent from congregational prayers. Article 61 of the Church Order suggests that congregational prayer include "adoration, confession, thanksgiving, supplication, and intercession for all Christendom and all humanity."

58. Overseeing the Administration of the Sacraments

The sacraments—the Lord's Supper and baptism—are essential parts of the worship service. They prominently fit the dialogue pattern described in the previous section. In holy communion Christ offers himself sacramentally to the congregation, and the congregation eats and drinks in faithful response. In baptism the water signs (symbolizes) and seals (guarantees) the grace and promises of God in Jesus Christ.

The sacraments were given by Christ to the church for strengthening the faith of believers. While the gospel itself brings the message of salvation and, by God's grace, changes hearts, the sacraments are instituted by the Lord to portray and seal these realities of salvation. In that sense, the sacraments are an added gift: what the gospel promises, the sacraments confirm in a visible, tangible way.

The sacraments are administered upon the authority of the consistory in a public worship service by a minister of the Word or by an evangelist. Word and sacrament belong together (Church Order, Art. 55).

> Helpful reading regarding the sacraments:
>
> - Articles 55-60 of the Church Order.
>
> - Synodical studies found in the *Acts of Synod 1991*, pp. 706-707; and the *Agenda for Synod 1994*, pp. 166-191.
>
> - Forms for baptism and the Lord's Supper in the *Psalter Hymnal*.
>
> - Lord's Days 25-27 of the Heidelberg Catechism; Articles 33 and 34 of the Belgic Confession, and *Our World Belongs to God*, paragraph 37.

Baptism

▶ In infant baptism God seals his covenant promises to the children of believers. It is the sacred duty of parents to present their children for baptism without unnecessary delay. Adopted children shall also have the privilege of baptism. Parents should faithfully explain to their children the meaning and implications of their baptism. Children of at least one believing parent, having been born in the covenant, receive the sacrament of baptism as a sign and seal which assures them, as they grow up, that God will not fail them.

- Youth or adults who have not been baptized shall receive holy baptism upon public profession of faith. The form for the Baptism of Adults shall be used for such public professions. New believers, having been saved by grace through faith—which is the entrance into the church—receive baptism as a sign and seal that the Lord will not fail them and that Satan cannot pluck them out of God's hand.

- Synod disapproved of rebaptism of adults, stating that such practice "is not in accord with the teaching of Scripture and the confessions" (*Acts of Synod 1971*, p. 162).

- Synod pronounced itself against the idea of baptism with the Holy Spirit as a "second blessing." It appealed to 1 Corinthians 12:13: "For we were all baptized by one Spirit into one body . . . and were all given the one Spirit to drink." Synod also appealed to Ephesians 2:18, 22; John 3:5; Acts 2:39; Romans 8:1-17; 15:13; 1 Corinthians 3:16; 2 Corinthians 1:21; Galatians 3:2; 5:16-26; and 1 John 2:20-27.

- Church Order Article 58 states, "The baptism of one who comes from another Christian denomination shall be held valid if it has been administered in the name of the triune God, by someone authorized by that denomination."

The Lord's Supper

- Article 60 of the Church Order states that the Lord's Supper shall be administered at least once every three months. However, Synod 1971 encouraged the churches to celebrate the supper more often (*Acts of Synod 1971*, p. 131). Article 60 also states: "The consistory shall provide for such administrations as it shall judge most conducive to edification. However, the ceremonies as prescribed in God's Word shall not be changed" (see also the Belgic Confession, Art. 35 and the Heidelberg Catechism, Lord's Days 28-30). Methods of supervising the supper are left up to the consistory (*Acts of Synod 1975*, p. 103).

- Guests who are communicant members in good standing of a Christian church may be invited to partake but should be informed of the requirements for participation: repentance, faith, and a desire for godly living (*Acts of Synod 1975*, p.103). This does not mean that participants may not have problems or even struggles of faith. The very institution of Holy Communion was aimed at strengthening those weak in the faith.

- The sick should be encouraged to receive the Lord's Supper at home from a representative of the congregation (*Acts of Synod 1914*, p. 17).

- May children attend the Lord's Supper? Yes, upon "an appropriate examination concerning their motives, faith, and life" before their age-appropriate public profession of faith. When those who have made that profession reach eighteen years of age, they shall be invited to make a further commitment to the creeds of the Christian Reformed Church and the responsibilities of adult membership and be accorded the full rights and privileges of such membership (*Acts of Synod 1995*, p. 762; Art. 59b).

Humble Gratitude

Isn't it embarrassing that Christians over the centuries were so bitterly divided over the sacraments—these special gifts of Christ to comfort the fainthearted—that they fought wars over them and divided churches over them? Our hearts should overflow with gratitude for these gifts of love from God. At the same time, we should be careful not to impose our strong opinions on others who disagree with us. The Word of God does not give many details about the exact nature of the sacraments. These gifts came with a minimum of explanation.

In response, your council can do at least two things:

- Teach the congregation to be grateful for the riches of the sacraments and to use them in faith and reverence. For example, the Lord's Supper is more than a memorial; it is a "spiritual table at which Christ communicates himself to us with all his benefits" (Belgic Confession, Art. 35).

- Head off any disputes over the meaning and practice of the sacraments.

The Sacrament of the Lord's Supper

We believe that our good God,
mindful of our crudeness and weakness,
has ordained sacraments for us

> to seal his promises in us,
> to pledge his good will and grace toward us,
> and also to nourish and sustain our faith . . . .
> confirming in us
> the salvation he imparts to us . . . .
> although the manner in which he does it
> goes beyond our understanding
> and is incomprehensible to us . . . .

Yet we do not go wrong when we say
that what is eaten is Christ's own natural body
and what is drunk is his own blood—
but the manner in which we eat it
is not by the mouth but by the Spirit,
through faith.

—*from the Belgic Confession, Articles 33 and 35*

59. Using the Heidelberg Catechism in Preaching

Article 54b of the Church Order says, "At one of the services each Lord's Day, the minister shall ordinarily preach the Word as summarized in the Heidelberg Catechism, following its sequence."

Note some implications:

▶ The word "ordinarily" is used to avoid rigidity. Exceptions may be made.

▶ Note the phrase "in sequence." Don't skip through the Heidelberg Catechism at random. Congregations will profit from a systematic study of the catechism. Devote the second service to its exposition and you will find that attendance will increase!

▶ Note also that the phrase "preach the catechism" does not appear in the Church Order. The catechism is a summary and interpretation of the Word of God—a human formulation that is not equal to the Word. The Word is preached; the preaching of the Word is aided by the catechism.

▶ There are at least two advantages to using the catechism regularly:

1. It helps preachers deal with the main themes of salvation as the catechism gleans them from the Word. Thus it keeps preachers from becoming one-sided, dwelling too much on their own choices as to what is important.

2. The catechism has helped to create in the churches a common understanding of the doctrines of salvation and the godly walk of life. Synod 1950 suggested that the classical church visitors ensure that the catechism is being used seriously. Synod then added the stipulation that the "division to be preached [be] read to the congregation before the sermon is preached" (*Acts of Synod 1950*, p. 441).

▶ Synod encouraged the churches also to use the Belgic Confession and the Canons of Dort in preaching (*Acts of Synod 1973*, p. 65). Admittedly, this stipulation of the Church Order has been overlooked in many congregations. Elders and pastors would be wise to discuss how this should be honored in your congregation.

60. Supporting Missions and Evangelism

Why do mission? Because mission is the heart of God.

Mission and evangelism begin with God's loving, forgiving heart for his people. In Genesis 3:8 we see God in the Garden of Eden, seeking Adam and Eve even though they have turned from him in sin. Beginning in that moment, God is seeking a restored love relationship with his people. God's ultimate action to reconcile our broken relationships was sending Jesus. Jesus' death and resurrection made a right relationship with the Father possible.

The Father sent the Son. The Son sent the Holy Spirit. The Father, Son, and Holy Spirit send us as Jesus' disciples. The mission of the church is to participate in God's desire for a restored relationship with his people and his creation.

God's desire is made very clear in the Great Commission: "Go and make disciples of all nations" (Matt. 28:19; see also Mark 16:15-18; Luke 24:45-49; John 17:18; 20:21-23; Acts 1:8; 2 Cor. 5:18-21).

The Christian Reformed Church is a mission church. The denomination has carefully defined the mission challenge for the church at the local, classical, and synodical level. In doing so the denomination is responding to God's mission heart.

The Elder's Role in Evangelism and Mission

In Articles 73-77 of the Church Order the denomination spells out a number of basic provisions, giving this mission vision flesh and blood.

Councils have an important responsibility in leading their churches to obey the Great Commission. The Church Order stipulates that "each council shall stimulate the members of the congregation to be witnesses for Christ in word and deed and to support the work of home and foreign missions by their interest, prayers, and gifts" (Art. 73b). It also states that ministers and elders shall "engage in and promote the work of evangelism" (Art. 12a). In the form for the Ordination of Elders and Deacons, leaders are challenged to "share with all the good news of salvation."

The Heidelberg Catechism and Mission

Lord's Day 21, Answer 54 states the challenge eloquently:

I believe that the Son of God
    through his Spirit and Word,
    out of the entire human race,
    from the beginning of the world to its end,
gathers, protects, and preserves for himself
    a community chosen for eternal life
    and united in true faith.

The Contemporary Testimony and Mission

In *Our World Belongs to God*, paragraph 41, we read:

Joining the mission of God,
the church is sent
with the gospel of the kingdom
to call everyone to know and follow Christ
and to proclaim to all
the assurance that in the name of Jesus
there is forgiveness of sin
and new life for all who repent and believe.
The Spirit calls all members
to embrace God's mission
in their neighborhoods
and in the world:
to feed the hungry,
bring water to the thirsty,
welcome the stranger,
clothe the naked,
care for the sick,
and free the prisoner.
We repent of leaving this work to a few,
for this mission is central to our being.

The practice of evangelism, if it is to be consistent and productive, must spring from the heart of your congregation. What does that look like? It starts with a love relationship. A congregation that has experienced God's salvation through Jesus will be compelled to share it with others.

Here are some ways elders can support the church's mission and evangelism efforts:

▶ Examine your own relationship with God. Have you experienced God's reconciling love for you in Jesus Christ? If you have, let this experience stir your heart for evangelism.

▶ Encourage an atmosphere where people hear the good news of the gospel. Is the gospel regularly presented at worship or on other occasions? How can you encourage that?

▶ Encourage discipleship. A church that expects evangelistic growth must be prepared to train disciples. How are people encouraged to grow in knowledge of Jesus and the Word? How can you encourage and support that activity?

▶ Many churches have a mission statement that guides the work of missions of the church. Does yours express God's evangelistic mission? If it's not emphatic enough, lead a process of revisiting your congregation's vision/ mission statement.

▶ Pray for your congregation's mission. Prayer connects us to the heart of God and leads the work. Encourage your church to develop and implement a prayer strategy for mission. This is not a quick fix. It takes time and energy to build a praying church and to see the fruit of those prayers in a congregation.

▶ Support the evangelistic efforts with the budget of your church. Your church may need to hire staff or host events to train and support evangelistic efforts.

▶ Pray for unbelievers in your circle of relationships. Value and nurture relationships with them.

▶ Model a welcoming atmosphere by having conversations with people outside your circle at church. Warmly enfold those who have a different ethnicity, church experience, or physical ability.

▶ Support your church's evangelistic events by attending and participating. It is discouraging to those doing the work when the elders do not support it. It is motivating when elders attend and add a "Good job!"

▶ Encourage those in your church who have evangelistic gifts. These people connect their lives to others by serving, praying, and speaking about faith. Celebrate their contribution and support them.

World Missions

God's mission heart also extends into the world. The Christian Reformed Church has had a long love of world missions. Way back in 1910, synod listed half a dozen ways that local churches could support the cause of the worldwide spread of the gospel.

Synod pointed to preaching and teaching as prime avenues to instill the missionary spirit in their members. It challenged each church to sponsor its own missionary and hold regular mission festivals. Synod also proposed that "systematic weekly offerings be taken for missions" (*Acts of Synod 1910*, p. 24). Good advice! God has richly blessed the missionary efforts of the Christian Reformed Church.

They Will Gladly Help

For helpful advice, assistance, and resources, contact Christian Reformed World Missions, Christian Reformed Home Missions, Back to God Ministries International, Faith Alive Christian Resources, and Christian Reformed World Relief Committee. (For addresses, see pp. 179 and 180.)

Beyond the
Local Church

In the last part of this manual we will explore
the larger context in which God has placed your
church. What is your relationship to other churches
of the denomination and, beyond that, with other
expressions of the Christian faith in our world?

Part 5

61. Being Part of Classis

The Christian Reformed Church knows three basic assemblies: the *council* of a congregation, the *classis*, and the *synod* (Church Order, Art. 26). We've already talked about the council, and we'll look at the synod in section 63, so in this part we'll focus on the classis.

The church of Christ is broader than the local congregation. Through classis, congregations enjoy fellowship, encourage and help each other, and are mutually accountable.

A classis consists of delegates from a group of about twenty churches located in a certain geographic area (Art. 39). The Christian Reformed Church is composed of forty-seven classes—twelve in Canada and thirty-six in the United States (Classis Lake Superior has congregations on both sides of the border). Each classis sends four delegates (two ministers and two elders) to the one-week meeting of the annual synod.

The churches agreed that classes should confine their work to two areas: matters that the congregations have in common and matters that the local council cannot finish by itself (Art. 28b).

Churches in a particular classis might, for instance, work together to open a chaplaincy ministry at a nearby university campus if such a project is too big for one church. Or a council may be faced with an internal conflict that it finds difficult to solve, so it turns to classis, which may appoint a task force to provide assistance. Classes have also been instrumental in establishing new churches.

In order to understand the authority by which classis does its work, we must first go to the local church. The church has a council that governs with the authority of Christ. The Church Order calls it *original authority* (Art. 27a). Classis and synod are expressions of the broader unity of the church. They do their ministry, each in its assigned domain, with the same authority as the local council. The Church Order calls this *delegated authority* since these assemblies are composed of delegates (Art. 27a). However, a classis has authority over a local council, just as synod has authority over the classes (Art. 27b).

Following are a few more details you may wish to note regarding your classis:

- Each church delegates a minister and an elder to represent the church at classis. When a church is without a pastor, two elders are delegated (Art. 40a). Synod 1997 and 2007 agreed that local councils may also add a deacon to the delegation. But each classis has the right to decide whether it will accept deacon-delegates as a matter of policy (Supplement Art. 40a). If a local council is unable to send an elder delegate, it may send a deacon. Classis will then vote whether to seat the deacon with voting rights. Newly ordained elders are encouraged to attend classis meetings as observers to get a feel for the work.

- Classis elects its own president, who serves only for that session. A rotation system may be used, but no one may be president twice in a row (Art. 40c). Classis also has a stated clerk and a treasurer. They continue their function even when a classis is not in session. Their duties are outlined in Article 32.

- Classis meetings are open to visitors, except when classis meets in "executive session." Officebearers who are not delegates may be given an "advisory voice" (Art. 40a).

- Classis, as well as the local church, must be properly incorporated. You may wish to make sure that your church is properly incorporated. (See *Acts of Synod 1963*, p. 51; *Acts of Synod 1997*, pp. 616-620. Model forms for incorporation of churches in the United States and Canada may also be found on the CRCNA website.)

- The local council must provide its classis delegates with proper credentials authorizing them to participate in the work of classis (Art. 34). Classical credential forms are available from Faith Alive Christian Resources. Log on to www.FaithAliveResources.org and search for "classical credential."

- Classis is a deliberative body (Art. 34). Its members vote on matters after due deliberation, information, discussion, and debate. That's why councils do not bind their delegates to vote a certain way. It is, of course, a council's privilege to send a communication to classis explaining its position on an issue coming before classis. The delegates of that council, once they have had the benefit of the discussion, may actually vote against their own council's proposal, though this is not likely.

- The denomination feels so strongly about the church's calling in the areas of evangelism/missions and mercy that it requires classes to have a classical home missions committee and a classical diaconal committee (Art. 75).

▶ Because preparing gifted young members for the ministry is important, classes must maintain a student fund to assist them (Art. 21).

▶ The business of classes, between meetings, is administered by the Classical Interim Committee (in some classes that committee goes by another name).

▶ A congregation may transfer from one classis to another. One of the two classes must approve the request. Synod also has to give its approval.

▶ Local churches normally relate to synod through their classis. Overtures, appeals, and communications to synod are carefully considered by classis for its possible support and processing.

62. Welcoming Classical Church Visitors

It is a time-honored custom in the Christian Reformed Church: once a year classis sends a delegation of two officebearers to visit with all the councils of the churches in the classis (Art. 42).

On behalf of the other churches the visitors come to see how each church in the classis is doing. They bring encouragement, speak words of advice and commendation, and take note of God's blessings.

The Church Order outlines five main areas that should be covered in the visit (see sidebar). However, synods were so concerned about the substance of the visit that they drafted a broader set of questions for the church visitors to ask. As more issues arose, more questions were added. Now there are almost fifty questions.

Article 42b of the Church Order states,

"The church visitors shall ascertain whether the officebearers faithfully perform their duties, adhere to sound doctrine, observe the provisions of the Church Order, and properly promote the edification of the congregation and the extension of God's kingdom. They shall admonish those who have been negligent, and help all with advice and assistance."

The intention was noble, but church visitors are now often under much pressure to finish the visit in time. Moreover, formal questions tend to solicit formal answers. Many church visits have turned into a probing examination rather than a meeting of hearts. Church visiting, however, is a fine institution and deserves to be preserved.

How the Church Visitors Function

▶ Church visitors should take note of the questions prescribed in the Church Order, make a mental summary of the subjects, determine which apply to the council they are to visit, and cover the material briefly with the council members. The larger part of the visit should focus on a discussion of the well-being of the church and its council.

▶ The council should set the meeting's agenda. Its members should tell of struggles, disappointments, and setbacks, but also of progress, victories, and growth. In response, the church visitors will listen, empathize, encourage, and advise. They will lead in meaningful prayer. Local officebearers should make the visit a matter of prayer and reflect carefully on what they wish to report to the church visitors (*Acts of Synod 1936*, pp. 122-123).

▶ Classis may send two ministers or one minister and one elder as visitors. Synod said that the visitors have to be "experienced and competent officebearers" (Art. 42a). Most classes appoint two or more teams.

▶ Synod said that the visit should be made once a year (Art. 42a). In some classes the visits are made only once every two or three years. If these visits are to be truly helpful, the councils should probably insist on an annual visit (*Acts of Synod 1975*, p. 17). The upcoming visit should be announced to all council members and to the congregation.

▶ Councils may also invite the church visitors to help when serious problems arise (Art. 42c).

▶ The church visitors submit a written report of their work to classis (Art. 42d).

63. Being Part of Synod

It is likely that some of your elders have attended synod. They will probably remember it as a demanding but rewarding experience. Synod is not only a deliberative body; it is also an occasion for learning.

Synod meets once a year (Art. 46a). Articles 45-50 of the Church Order outline the structure and function of synod.

The Composition and Function of Synod

▶ Synod is composed of four delegates from each classis—two ministers and two elders. They represent the churches of their classis (Art. 45). Synod elects four officers—a president, a vice president, a first clerk, and a second clerk. (Most classes are prepared to compensate elder delegates for loss of wages when needed.)

▶ Synod deals with matters that concern all the churches and matters that the classes cannot finish (Art. 28b). The Church Order outlines six areas in which synods do basic work: adoption of the creeds, of the Church Order, of liturgical forms, of the *Psalter Hymnal,* and of principles and elements of the order of worship, as well as the designation of Bible versions to be used in worship (Art. 47).

▶ Synod also supervises a variety of denominational ministries: Back to God Ministries International, Calvin College, Calvin Theological Seminary, Christian Reformed Home Missions, Christian Reformed World Missions, Christian Reformed World Relief Committee, Faith Alive Christian Resources and World Literature Ministries, Ministers' Pension Fund, and such pastoral ministries as Safe Church Ministry (formerly Abuse Prevention), Chaplaincy Ministries, Disability Concerns, Pastor-Church Relations, Race Relations, Social Justice, and others.

▶ Synod is assisted in the work of supervision by the denominational Board of Trustees. In order to facilitate its work, synod often appoints study committees, which may take two or more years to work on their assignments. Synod's overall responsibilities are also aided by several permanent service committees (previously called "standing committees").

▶ A program committee, composed of the officers of the previous synod, drafts the agenda of the upcoming synod. The program committee also appoints the advisory committees from the list of delegates well before the actual meeting of synod and assigns agenda material to each.

▶ The denomination's executive director, the director of denominational ministries, the director of finance and administration, the director of Canadian ministries, the presidents of Calvin College and Calvin Theological Seminary, and the seminary faculty serve as functionaries and advisers of synod on matters pertaining to their expertise.

▶ Annually, synod sets the amount that the churches are asked to contribute toward the denominational ministries. This amount is called "ministry shares" (previously called "quota").

By what authority does synod do its work? The Church Order gives the following summary: "Each assembly exercises . . . the ecclesiastical authority entrusted to the church by Christ; the authority of councils being original, that of major assemblies being delegated." Also, "the classis has the same authority over the council as the synod has over the classis" (Art. 27). That's why the work of synods should be respected and appreciated. Synod 1991 has rightly noted that movements and actions that undermine the authority of assemblies—be they council, classis, or synod—bring great harm to the unity of the church (*Acts of Synod 1991*, pp. 812-814).

"Settled and Binding"

To what extent are officebearers bound by synodical pronouncements and actions? Synodical "deliverances" are not at the same authority level as the confessions of the church. Still, Article 29 of the Church Order states that the decisions of assemblies are "considered settled and binding, unless it is proved that they conflict with the Word of God or the Church Order."

A denomination cannot hope to function fruitfully and effectively if common agreements are ignored at will. That does not mean that individual officebearers cannot feel unhappy with certain synodical expressions or actions.

Keep in mind that synodical deliverances stem from a large variety of problems, needs, opportunities, and situations. When synod interprets a creedal statement, adherence is much more consequential than an instance of synodical advice addressing a pastoral concern.

Synod once pointed out that each synodical decision has its own "use and function," which is clearly reflected by the very wording of each decision (pronouncements about creeds, expressions of the faith, adjudications, testimonies, guidelines for ministries and actions, pastoral advice, organizational regulations, and so on). The weight and consequences of an officebearer's disagreement are affected by all these situational nuances (*Acts of Synod 1975*, pp. 44-46).

Church leaders should, however, always be aware that the responsibilities and privileges of their offices necessitate a healthy respect for synodical deliverances. The church, therefore, has always expected officebearers not to express their differences in teaching and writing, nor to agitate for noncompliance.

64. Being Part of the Worldwide Church

We are thankful for the Christian Reformed Church and the Reformed faith. We are equally thankful for the multitude of Christian churches around the world that form with us the worldwide Church of Christ. God promised Abraham that through his descendents all nations would be blessed. Where that unity of all believers becomes visible, we rejoice.

The Belgic Confession speaks of that vision eloquently:

> And so this holy church
> is not confined,
> bound,
> or limited to a certain place or certain persons.
> But it is spread and dispersed
> throughout the entire world,
>   though still joined and united
>   in heart and will,
>   in one and the same Spirit,
>   by the power of faith. (Art. 27)

The CRC adopted a new Ecumenical Charter in 2006 (*Agenda for Synod 2006*, pp. 298ff.) in which the vision for the worldwide body of believers is spelled out. The possibilities of practicing fellowship and cooperation with other Christian church bodies are a continuation of the CRCNA's traditional policies (*Acts of Synod 1985*, pp. 205, 237-241; *Acts of Synod 1987*, pp. 587-591; *Acts of Synod 1988*, pp. 562-564).

There are now two categories of bilateral relationships with other churches (*Acts of Synod 2006*, pp. 302, 303):

▶ Churches in ecclesiastical fellowship—with these churches we exchange fraternal delegates at major assemblies, share in communion around the Lord's Table, join in common actions, and communicate on issues of joint concern. These denominations are found not only on this continent but in countries in Latin America, Asia, Europe, Africa, and Australia.

▶ Churches in dialogue—with these churches we maintain contact with a view to exploring cooperation.

The Christian Reformed Church holds that biblical truth must be cherished, but also that unity itself is an expression of truth and a gift of Christ (see John 17; 1 Cor. 12; Eph. 4; and Lord's Day 21 of the Heidelberg Catechism).

Our denomination currently holds membership in four national ecumenical organizations:

▶ The Evangelical Fellowship of Canada

▶ The Canadian Council of Churches

▶ The National Association of Evangelicals, USA.

▶ Christian Churches Together (newly formed in 2007, this is a platform that seeks to bring Protestants, Evangelicals, Pentecostals, Orthodox, and Catholic churches into conversation).

We also hold membership in two international organizations (which plan to merge in 2010 into one organization called World Communion of Reformed Churches)

▶ The Reformed Ecumenical Council (REC), gathering together leaders of thirty-nine denominations and comprising some 12.5 million Christians, is a close family of Reformed churches. High quality fellowship has been marked by deep discussions with participation of many African and Asian Reformed churches.

▶ The World Alliance of Reformed Churches (WARC), based in Geneva, is an older and larger body that first drew together major streams of Reformed and Presbyterian churches. With about 215 member churches comprising 70 million Christians, WARC has a platform to address world issues on behalf of the Reformed family.

Biblical ecumenical efforts have also taken place through many years in many places, as individual Christian Reformed congregations cooperated with other Christian groups. The beauty of ecumenism is that it opens our eyes to the great things Christ is doing in incredibly diversified settings, that it makes the unity we have with fellow believers around the world increasingly visible, and that we grow in appreciation for the treasures we possess in our local churches.

65. In Support of Christian Schools

The Christian Reformed Church has always been committed to Christian school education. Christian leaders from previous generations saw to it that leaders today would share the same commitment. "The council shall diligently encourage the members of the congregation to establish and maintain good Christian schools" (Church Order, Art. 71). Synods through the years confirmed that challenge by saying that our children are religious beings with spiritual needs. Synod also stated

▶ that education is the nurturing of the whole person in the fear of God which is the beginning of wisdom (*Acts of Synod 1898*, p. 38);

▶ that baptism is the sign of the covenant and that Christian education is part of covenantal living (*Acts of Synod 1951*, p. 44);

▶ that life knows of no separation between the sacred and the secular and that Christian education honors our King, who has been given dominion over all life's realms (*Acts of Synod 1955*, pp. 193-200; see also *Our World Belongs to God*, paragraph 47).

What Can Councils Do?

▶ Keep the issue of Christian day school education before the congregation. The Church Order uses the word "encourage." In an edifying way let your members know that Christian education is dear to you as spiritual leaders. Pastors deserve the elders' support when they express that vision from the pulpit. Elders who do not send their children to a Christian school can still support the principle of Christian schools.

▶ On a personal basis, encourage Christian school teachers in your church circles. Show your interest in their work and well-being. And don't forget the Christian school board members. All these people must fulfill an awesome task with limited means. Stop by your nearby schools now and then. Attend Christian school events, even when you have no children in school. Encourage Christian teachers and administrators in public schools to express a Christian testimony in their schools when possible.

- As a council, ensure that your church has funds available for parents who lack sufficient financial resources to meet tuition costs. Encourage all your members to give their financial support.

- If there are no Christian schools from a Reformed perspective in your area, elders can serve parents by helping them select the most appropriate Christian schools from other Christian traditions.

- It is important that congregations foster a deep concern for all the children in the community by praying regularly for the public schools in the area and supporting excellent education in them.

66. Relating to Parachurch Organizations

In Canada and the United States there are scores of religious and charitable organizations and advocacy groups. Local church councils are regularly approached by these organizations for financial support and sometimes for endorsement.

It is not easy for councils to define a set of guidelines to assist them in making responsible and intelligent choices, but here are some observations that may serve you:

▶ Synods have pointed out regularly that the denomination's own ministries ought to have the churches' priority when requests for aid are considered. Among them are ministries in the area of evangelism, missions, mercy, and Christian education whose programs are only partially supported by ministry shares. Every year synod lists these causes in the *Acts of Synod* and sends lists to the church treasurers. Synod recommends these causes for "one or more offerings." Synod adds a special list for some youth causes.

▶ It should be noted that denominational agencies are often more cost-effective in delivering ministry per dollar than parachurch organizations that have to spend a great deal of money on fundraising.

▶ Synods have also maintained contact with scores of nondenominational organizations and have recommended them to the churches for support. Their names are also listed in the *Acts of Synod* under three headings: benevolent agencies, educational agencies, and miscellaneous agencies. Separate lists are drawn up for the United States and Canada.

▶ The organizations listed there submit full reports of their ministries and financial dealings to synod, and are annually reviewed by synod's Board of Trustees. Since more than forty organizations are mentioned, local churches have plenty of choices. You can be confident that your gift is put to good use by any of these organizations. You may not have that certainty with organizations not mentioned on synod's list.

▶ There are many organizations that are active in areas not mentioned on synod's list. If you feel deeply about their mission and feel inclined to support them, by all means check them out. Ask them to send you their annual report, their budget, and their financial report, and ask specifically which proportions of your support dollar go for promotion, for administration, and for actual ministry.

▶ You will probably be approached by local causes. Your council members may know something about the values and ministry of these organizations. But it's appropriate to do some research as well. You may conclude that these causes merit your support since they meet needs in an area of interest to you. Life would be unlivable for many people across the continent without such organizations.

Since available support funds are limited, you may wish to give the denominational causes and causes related to the denomination your top priority.

On the other hand, we are grateful that in this broken and needy world there are many organizations that do good work and bring solace and relief to those who suffer. Follow the dictates of your heart, but also follow your head: can it be demonstrated that recommending them for support is warranted? If so, do it wholeheartedly.

In Conclusion: Godspeed!

"Of making many books there is no end, and much study wearies the body" (Eccles. 12:12).

Must you go by the book as you work as an elder? I would not answer that question with a resounding "yes." You are called, foremost, to be a shepherd. You have a shepherd's heart. In the company of the great Shepherd, follow his dictates.

Church life comes with so many unpredictable situations, so many problems for which there are no easy solutions, so much pain for which there seems to be no solace. On many occasions you find yourself improvising, but amid the complexities of congregational realities you will be able to find some guideposts on the preceding pages.

> "Now may the God of peace, who through the blood of the eternal covenant brought back from the dead our Lord Jesus, that great Shepherd of the sheep, equip you with everything good for doing his will, and may he work in us what is pleasing to him, through Jesus Christ, to whom be glory for ever and ever, Amen."
>
> —Hebrews 13:20-21

Topical Index

Appendix

Denominational Offices, Ministries and Agencies, and Publications

Church council members will find a wealth of helpful resources with the denominational ministries of the Christian Reformed Church.

Denominational offices

Christian Reformed Church in North America (U.S. office)

2850 Kalamazoo Ave. SE
Grand Rapids, Mich. 49560
616-241-1691 or 877-279-9994 (toll free)
www.crcna.org

Christian Reformed Church in North America (Canada office)

3475 Mainway, PO Box 5070 STN LCD 1
Burlington , ON L7R 3Y8
905-336-2920 or 800-730-3490 (toll free)
www.crcna.org

Executive Director: 616-224-0832
Director of Denominational Ministries: 616-224-0744
Director of Canadian Ministries: 905-336-2920

Agencies and Ministries
Back to God Ministries International

Grand Rapids office: 616-224-0804; 877-279-9994
Palos Heights office: 708-371-8700; 800-879-6555
www.btgh.org

Calvin Institute of Christian Worship

616-526-6088
www.calvin.edu/worship

Center for Excellence in Preaching

616-957-6085

http://cep.calvinseminary.edu

Chaplaincy Ministries

616-224-0844

www.crcna.org/chaplaincy

Christian Reformed Home Missions

616-224-0722; 800-266-2175

www.crhm.org

Christian Reformed World Missions

U.S. office: 616-224-0700; 800-346-0075

Canada office: 905-336-2920

www.crwm.org

Christian Reformed World Relief Committee

U.S. office: 616-224-0740

Canada office: 905-336-2920

www.crwrc.org

Disability Concerns

U.S. office: 616-224-0844; 888-463-0272

Canada office: 905-336-2920; 800-730-3490

www.crcdisabilityconcerns.org

Faith Alive Christian Resources

616-224-0819; 800-333-8300

www.FaithAliveResources.org

Friendship Ministries

2215 29th St. SE #B6

Grand Rapids, MI 49508

616-301-7729; 888-866-8966

www.friendship.org

Ministerial Information Service

see Pastor-Church Relations Service

Pastor-Church Relations Service
616-224-0746
www.crcna.org/pages/pastorchurch.cfm

Race Relations
616-224-5883
www.crcna.org/race

Safe Church Ministry
616-224-0735
www.crcna.org/safechurch

Youth Unlimited (includes Cadets and GEMS)
1333 Alger St. SE
Grand Rapids, MI 49507
616-241-5616
www.youthunlimited.org

Publications
The Banner
616-224-0731
www.TheBanner.org

Church Order and Rules for Synodical Procedure
This booklet is updated annually in booklet form and mailed to all CRC church councils.
It is also available from Faith Alive Christian Resources.
www.FaithAliveResources.org

A Compassionate Journey: Coming Alongside People with Disabilities or Chronic Illnesses
John G. Cook
Available from Faith Alive Christian Resources.

The Compassionate Congregation: A Handbook for People Who Care
Karen Mulder and Ginger Jurries
Available from Faith Alive Christian Resources.

The Empty Pew—Caring for Those who Leave
Louis M. Tamminga
Available from Faith Alive Christian Resources.

Finding the Right Pastor for Your Church
Dirk J. Hart
Available from Pastor-Church Relations.

Just One Click: Christians, Porn, and the Lure of Cybersex
Robert J. Baird and Ronald L. Vanderbeck
Available from Faith Alive Christian Resources.

Manual of Christian Reformed Church Government, 2008 edition, Peter Borgdorff
Available from Faith Alive Christian Resources.

The Ministry of the Elder
Robert White
Available from Faith Alive Christian Resources.

Moving Your Church Through Conflict
Speed B. Leas
Purchase a downloadable file from the Alban Institute at www.alban.org.

Pastoral Care for Homosexual Members (A summary of the 1973 and 2002 synodical study reports)
Louis M. Tamminga
Available from Faith Alive Christian Resources.

Pastoral Care—In Life and in Death—A Pastoral Guide for Funerals
Leonard Vander Zee
Available from Faith Alive Christian Resources.

Preventing Child Abuse
Beth Swagman
Available from Faith Alive Christian Resources.

Principles of Drug Addiction Treatment—A Research-Based Guide

This helpful pamphlet is offered by the National Institute on Drug Abuse. To order, log on to http://www.nida.nih.gov/podat/PODATIndex.html.

Reformed—What It Means, Why It Matters

Robert De Moor

Available from Faith Alive Christian Resources.

Reformed Worship

Resources for planning and leading worship.

Published quarterly by Faith Alive Christian Resources.

www.ReformedWorship.org

So You've Been Asked to Make Visits

Louis M. Tamminga

Available from Faith Alive Christian Resources.

Worship study reports

Acts of Synod 1928, pp. 276-302; *Acts of Synod 1930*, pp. 335-353; and *Acts of Synod 1968*, pp. 134-198.